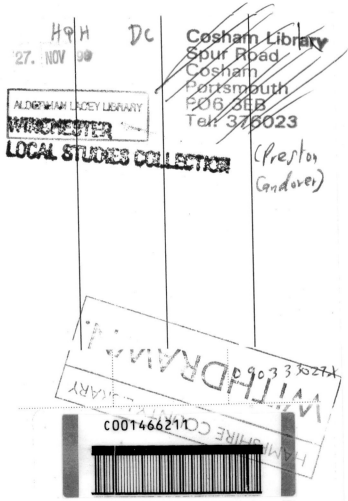

A Downland Village

PORTRAIT OF A HAMPSHIRE PARISH

PHILIP SHEAIL

BARRY SHURLOCK

Winchester

BARRY SHURLOCK
& Co. (Publishers) Ltd
174 *Stockbridge Road*
Winchester
Hants, SO22 6RW

© *Philip Sheail* 1979
First published 1979

ISBN 0 903330 27 X

Made in Great Britain by
The Pitman Press Ltd
Bath

Contents

Preface

The material for *A Downland Village* has been collected intermittently over the past fifteen years or more, and during this time I have had the assistance of many people, especially my grandfather, Mr W. Murphy. Sadly though, two people who made the greatest contribution are no longer with us—first, Canon C. Bryan who gave me unlimited access to the parish records which he then held, and whose parish magazine *Oxdrove* enabled several people to record their memories of village life. And secondly, the most notable contributor to the *Oxdrove*, the late Mrs D. D. Cosier, who always gave me every assistance in my researches. During her long life in Preston, she gathered many stories about the village and these anecdotes of particular characters and events have proved invaluable.

During the writing of this book I have been assisted by many people who have provided certain information in particular Sir H. A. C. Rumbold, Bart; Mr M. Baker, the Archivist of Wellington College; Mr J. Macfarlane and Mr V. Drabble of Utah, U.S.A.; and the County Archivist and staff of the Hampshire Record Office. As regards the photographs, I have to thank the Norfolk County Library for providing the portrait of Charles Rumbold; Mr J. L. Jervoise of Herriard Park for making available certain portraits of the Jervoise family, and Mr Brian Stewart for carrying out the necessary photography. Thanks for the loan of other photographs must go to the Reverend K. V. Batt of Preston Candover, Mr V. Drabble, and especially to Miss G. M. Coakes. I am also grateful for advice received from Mr John Arlott, Dr I. J. Sanderson, Mr E. Roberts, and especially from my brother, Dr John Sheail, who started the whole thing off in the early 1960s and has since given me many useful leads to sources of information. I have been most ably assisted by Dr and Mrs P. Skeggs and by my parents, Mr and Mrs F. Sheail, in the promotion of the book. Finally, I must thank my wife, Janet, whose assistance and encouragement have been largely responsible for bringing the venture to fruition at long last.

Philip Sheail
Hertford
August 78

1

Census Night 1851

Sunday evening, the thirtieth day of March 1851, was possibly the first time for a week that John Thorp had been able to relax. He was a butcher by trade but at that moment he was also serving as an Enumerator in the census of the population, and was responsible for the village of Preston Candover in Hampshire. His task consisted of giving out a special form to each household in the parish which had to be filled in on Sunday evening. During the next week he would collect up the completed forms, copy out the details into a special book, and then deliver it to the Registrar in Basingstoke. A body of civil servants would extract the figures they needed and then the book would be stored away with thousands of others in Somerset House. A census had taken place at ten-year intervals since 1801, but it was not until 1851 that it became really detailed and reliable. Thus when the book finally re-emerged for public viewing a hundred years later, it became possible for the first time in history to obtain an insight into the whole community of Preston Candover—from Mr Charles Rumbold of Preston House right down to Old Esther Adams, the village half-wit.

The census produced a kind of snapshot of each household as it was on that Sunday evening in 1851: Mr Rumbold, his family and staff as well as several guests, including the Reverend William Barnard, the local curate; the Allen family in the house behind the grocer's shop—Mrs Allen, her son George and his wife, and her niece, Ann Pinnock, who helped in the shop; Farmer John Lunn at Manor Farm, his family, his house servant,

Ann Wigg, and his six farm servants—William Munday, George Cull, James Brice, James Aslett, William Holdaway and George Large; Jack Thorn, a labourer living at the Old Marshes Farmhouse with his wife Harriet and their children—Maria, Elizabeth, James and Jane, as well as their young lodger, Tony Bulpitt. Two other Thorn children were living away from home that night: Ann, a servant for the village wood-dealer and Henry, a servant for an innkeeper and farmer at Ellisfield. Several Enumerators in the county came across other sons and daughters of Preston families: Mary Duffin visiting her married sister at Dummer; Charles Westbrook, an errand boy at the Black Boy Tavern in Basingstoke; Harriet Bramley, a servant for a miller and farmer at Neatham; Elizabeth Collins, a cook for the Rector of Lasham; Harriet Goodyear, a patient in the County Hospital at Winchester; and Henry Martin, a prisoner in the County gaol—sentenced on February 25th to two months imprisonment for 'offences against the game laws'.

A Downland Village sets out to explore Preston Candover together with the adjoining parish of Nutley in 1851 and in the decade on either side. Many documents have been consulted: primarily the Census of 1851 but also those of 1841 and 1861. Other sources include the Parish Registers, Rate Books, Highway Accounts, Vestry Minutes, Poor Law records, Directories, Burke's Peerage and Landed Gentry, various sales notices, court records and other items reported in the *Hampshire Chronicle*, and the copious historical notes left by the Reverend Sumner Wilson. To save space I have not given detailed references, but these will be available in a copy of the book to be deposited at the Hampshire Record Office.

Most of the sketches attempt to reconstruct the village scene in 1851 by using old photographs taken in the early 1900s together with maps of the period. Some guesswork has had to be used, of course, especially with such details as trees, hedges and fences. The photographs in the book are derived from portraits which survive from the 1850s and earlier, though these are mostly of the gentry. The majority of people must unfortunately remain faceless, although certain characters who lived in Preston in 1851 were photographed in the early 1900s and the best of these pictures have been included.

The period between 1840 and 1860 represented the early years of

2

Queen Victoria's reign, now mainly remembered by such famous names as Peel, Palmerston, Gladstone and Disraeli, and for such events as the Chartist riots, the Crimean War, the Indian Mutiny and the Great Exhibition in Hyde Park, the major event of 1851 which was no doubt visited by several inhabitants of Preston Candover. It was a time of great change—the towns and factories were expanding and the network of railways extending to all parts of the country. Soon the society of this Hampshire village would be affected by these changes, and the kind of community which John Thorp found on that March evening would disappear for ever.

The Candover Valley

The Reverend Sumner Wilson, who lived in Preston Candover for fifty-five years until his death in 1917, was an antiquarian in the grand old manner and spent much of his spare time studying the history of the parish. For some reason he never got round to putting his material in order but left it as a mass of notes and jottings, often written on the back of anything that came to hand: a price list from Dickins and Jones, or an application form for shares in the London and North Western Railway or in the Gwalla Copper Mines. Nonetheless, his researches were valuable in finding out how the village of his time had come into being.

The parish to which he devoted so much of his life lay within a broad valley in the chalk country of Central Hampshire. In the lowest reaches of the Valley near Alresford there flowed the Candover Brook, a tributary of the River Itchen, whose springs normally rose below Preston at a point between Brown and Chilton Candover. Thus in Preston parish and the higher country to the north, the downland valleys were quite devoid of any streams. The area had always been somewhat off the beaten track, lying at the centre of a triangle between Basingstoke, Alton and Winchester, and bypassed by all the main routes. People had been living in the valley, however, since very early times and Sumner Wilson avidly studied their remains: some worked flints on Budd's Hill, a tumulus at Bangor Copse, a Roman Villa in Chapel Field. The village of Preston Candover appeared to be Saxon in origin and was originally called *Prestecandevere*—the Candover belonging to the Priests—the name deriving from a religious community which had flourished there before the Norman Conquest. The parish which finally evolved from such misty origins comprised nearly 3,140 acres while its neighbour, the parish of Nutley, was about half this size. The name Nutley was derived apparently from 'the Lea where the nuts grew'. They were originally separate parishes lying within the Hundred of Bermondspit, but the Vicarages were amalgamated at the time of the Civil War and from then on their affairs were closely interlinked.

By later Saxon times the villages of Preston Candover and Nutley would have appeared as small settlements in the valley bottom, surrounded by large arable fields. Beyond the fields would be forest and open grazing land with tracks winding away to other villages. The peasants' cottages and crofts would be grouped around the church while at the end of the village would be the Manor House. About a couple of miles from Preston village some isolated homesteads stood on land carved out of the forest and these survived into later times as the farms of Moundsmere and Southwood. Then there was Axford, a hamlet lying on the Preston–Nutley border whose householders farmed land in both parishes.

By the eleventh century Preston parish had been carved up into six Manors whose Lords were carefully chronicled by Sumner Wilson: Hugh de Port, Ralph de Mortimer, William de Malduith, Matthew de Wallop, and many many more. The land from which they drew their revenues came to be organised in the medieval period on the common field system. This was based initially upon three large fields worked in common by the villagers, although new common fields might be added as the population grew. The fields of Preston and Nutley and the names by which they were later known are shown in the Map Section. Each field, which could be as much as two hundred acres in extent, was subdivided into bundles of strips called furlongs, each strip being ideally an acre in size. A family's holding would consist of a number of strips dotted about each of the common fields, and one example at Nutley is shown in the Map Section.

Much of the higher ground in the valley beyond the common fields was devoted to rough grazing land, also held in common—the Preston and Nutley Downs, Southwood Green and Oakhills Common. At one time Preston Down was joined to those of Brown and Chilton Candover, and was thus an ideal route for the drovers and their herds; the trackway

5

across the down is still known today as the Oxdrove. Elsewhere in the two parishes the villagers eventually ceased to create further strips at the edge of the common fields and instead each peasant began enclosing up to twenty acres of the waste for his own use. Many such 'ancient enclosures' were made during the late middle ages, carried out under the strict surveillance of the Lords of the Manor and their Courts.

The common field system long survived into a time when farming ceased to be quite so subsistent. Though surviving in name, the Lord of the Manor was replaced in the fifteenth and sixteenth centuries by the gentry, many of whom had made their wealth through trade. Below them were the Yeomanry who farmed the larger holdings of the parish and below them, the smallholders known as Husbandmen. At the very bottom was the class of landless labourers which grew steadily throughout the eighteenth century as a result of various economic forces, including the enclosure of the common fields.

Clearly, the scattered strips made farming very inefficient and their reorganisation into compact holdings had been taking place for many years, particularly where a whole parish was owned by one man. Where there was more than one owner, an Act of Parliament was often necessary and in the case of Preston and Nutley this finally came about in 1820. The Act treated both parishes as one and allowed for the enclosure of 1,800 acres of common field and down, though it excluded Oakhills Common. The tiny strips would be swept away and the land reallotted to all persons 'in proportion to their respective properties, rights of common and other interests in the same'. The Act also made it possible for people to exchange land outside the common fields, so as to achieve the most rational layout of farm holdings.

By the time of the enclosure some 78 per cent of land in the two parishes had come into the hands of just three landowners. There was now only one Lord of the Manor, George Purefoy Jervoise, who owned about 40 per cent of the total while Mr John Blackburn owned 26 per cent. Another 12 per cent belonged to the Wardens and Scholars of Winchester College whose lands mainly comprised the Moundsmere Estate. In the middle ages this land had been owned by a religious body, the Priory of Southwark, but following the dissolution of the monasteries, the estate had come eventually into the possession of Winchester College who in turn

6

leased it to one of the local landowners. In 1820 it was held by Jervoise. The Act mentioned 'divers other persons' whose interests would be safeguarded, but they carried little weight compared to Jervoise and Blackburn.

Once the Act was law, Mr George Barnes was appointed as Commissioner to put the enclosure into effect and a surveyor from Andover, William Walmsley, was engaged to carry out a survey of land holdings in both parishes. The Commissioner was then able to draw up a scheme for redividing the common lands which was argued over for many months. Finally, when agreement had been reached, the details were set down in a book called the Enclosure Award and this received its seal from the Clerk of the Peace at Winchester in August 1823.

The effect of the enclosure on the landscape of Preston and Nutley was enormous. The open arable fields and pasture were carved up by long straight fences, and the ancient strips soon ploughed out of existence. Thus by the 1850s only Oakhills remained as common land and consisted mostly of scrubby thickets which provided the poorer families with firewood and some grazing ground. It was to remain in this state until 1870 when it too was enclosed. The rest of the valley consisted mainly of well-ordered arable fields. The Award had stipulated that the new allotments must be hedged with hawthorn and these hedges were now fully established, but they still contrasted to the landscape of the ancient enclosures where the fields were usually smaller and where the hedges were not only thicker but composed of hazel and other shrubs and the occasional tree. Some pasture still remained on the Preston and Nutley Downs while the tops of the ridges were reserved for coppices. The old trackways still survived as the parish roads, although some changes had been made in the Award, especially on Preston Down, where the new roads often ran in a straight line and kept a wide verge or 'driftway' on one side so that the flocks of sheep would not disturb the road surface. Down nearer the village at the point where the old gates onto the common field had stood, the driftway stopped abruptly and the road continued as a narrow lane.

The village of Preston Candover formed a long straggle along the Turnpike in the valley bottom. For one traveller passing through in 1839, the most noteworthy features were the 'respectable gentlemen's houses',

Preston Candover, looking north from the village pond. On the right is the Croft; centre, the Forge Cottage, then the houses owned by George Allen and William Major

North and South Hall and Preston House. The largest farms lay on the roads leading out of the village while the church was right at the southern end with the rectory next door. The actual focal point of the village was the green, 20 rods in size, though Sumner Wilson claimed it had once been 2½ acres. For centuries a pond had lain at the fork of the Turnpike and the Wield Road, and on one side of it had stood a pound in which cattle had been impounded when their owners disobeyed the grazing rights on the common lands. It appears to have been removed soon after the enclosure. By the 1850s, therefore, although the spot still seems to have been called the green, it consisted only of the pond with its banks churned up by carts and hooves.

The cottages found through the village were a fair mixture of ages and styles. Some were sizeable houses, formerly the homes of yeomen farmers and possibly dating from the sixteenth century. A few had been constructed with a timber frame but the original wattle and daub walls had long been replaced by locally made bricks. In later houses the builders had dispensed with the timber frame altogether. Since 1800, however, the bricks had generally been used just to build up a framework, the walls between being filled in with flints. The roofs were of either thatch or tile.

8

Amongst the cottages were gardens, orchards, paddocks, pig-sties and chicken runs; two small farms, several trades and crafts, an endowed school, and a pub called the New Inn.

Preston village was by far the largest settlement in the locality. Axford was a hamlet of six cottages, two large farms and a smallholding. At Nutley village only a few buildings now remained: a small church, a farm called Nutley Manor, a couple of cottages, and the house of a former farm called Nutley Court which was split up into tenements for labourers and servants. Close to the Nutley border stood another tiny hamlet called Gobleyhole, which comprised three cottages standing on small round plots of land filched in the past from Nutley Down. A similar encroachment had occurred in another corner of the Down at a spot called Bermondspit and an isolated cottage stood here too.

By the year 1851, therefore, the two parishes contained a total of sixty-seven cottages, twelve farms and three mansions. In that year the census had recorded a total of 524 persons living in Preston, 169 in Nutley. They were arranged into a clearly defined class system which may be thought of as a pyramid. At the top were the families of the landed proprietor, clergy, and certain wealthy gentlemen who comprised 2 per cent of the population. The tenant farmers and their families comprised 7 per cent, while the shopkeepers, craftsmen and other tradesmen made up 15 per cent. The people in service amounted to 12 per cent. Finally, at the broad base of the pyramid were the families of the labouring class who comprised 64 per cent of the total population.

The Wield Road across Preston Down

For Sumner Wilson all this was very much the contemporary scene and his historical researches stopped well before the 1850s. Had he wished to describe the village of that time, he would no doubt have started with the class of people who to him were the most important—the wealthy individuals at the top of the pyramid who owned those 'respectable gentlemen's houses' and most of the parish as well.

3

The Landed Gentry

By the 1850s the chalk country of Hampshire had long been carved up
into a few large estates. Much of the country to the north and east of
Nutley was owned by the Earl of Portsmouth. The Rodneys owned parts
of Wield while the parishes of Northington, Swarraton, Brown and
Chilton Candover were the province of the Barings. Preston Candover
continued to be divided between several men, though by the 1850s there
were just two landed proprietors of any importance.

The largest estate was owned by the Jervoise family whose seat was actually outside the parish at Herriard Park. Their involvement in Preston
and Nutley had come about through the marriage in 1798 of George
Purefoy Jervoise to Elizabeth Hall. Her family had owned the Manor
Farms of Preston and Nutley for much of the eighteenth century. When
her father Thomas Hall died in 1812, there was no male heir to inherit the
estate so it passed to Elizabeth and thus into the hands of the Jervoises.
The latter had acquired Herriard Park early in the seventeenth century,
being already the Lords of the Manor of Britford near Salisbury. They
were important personalities in the County—George Purefoy Jervoise
served as High Sheriff in 1830 and was for some years Member of Parliament for Salisbury. He had been born in 1770 and had succeeded to the
Herriard estate in 1805, to which he thus added the Hall estates and later,
after Elizabeth's death in 1821, his marriage to a Miss Anna Wadham
Locke brought him another estate in Wiltshire.

Jervoise belonged to that respected class of men known as the 'resident native gentry'. His obituary in the *Hampshire Chronicle* in 1847 said of him:

> As a generous and considerate landlord, as a kind master, as the old English gentleman, exercising the hospitality that became his station—Mr Jervoise held a conspicuous place in the neighbourhood.

He also carried out many improvements. In Preston and Nutley his estate comprised three large farms and several smaller holdings, to which he added the bulk of the land owned by Winchester College held on a twenty-year lease. By 1814 he had had elegant farmhouses built at both Manor Farms and he was probably the main driving force behind the Enclosure Act. Disagreements with John Blackburn of Preston House made the redistribution of the common lands less than satisfactory, but this was not to be a problem for long as Blackburn died in 1824 and Jervoise was then able to buy up the pieces of land he wanted. In 1838 he carried out an exchange of land with the Preston House estate and this enabled him to have a completely new farmyard built in 1840 about a mile from the village on the Wield Road, which became known as The Down Farm. Thus by the 1840s the land he owned or leased amounted to 3,000 acres. He does not seem to have been as ruthless as some landowners, however, who concentrated their estates into a few large efficient farms, for most of the smaller holdings he had inherited were still in existence in the 1850s.

Jervoise also seems to have been more reasonable than many over the question of game. All the farms he owned in the two parishes were let to tenants, but he retained direct ownership over 300 acres of woodland and game coverts. Like most men of his class, he was a keen sportsman, a member of the Hampshire Hunt and owner of a pack of harriers. Many landowners at this time stopped their tenants from controlling the numbers of hares and rabbits despite the damage they might do to growing crops, but at Nutley Manor Farm Jervoise allowed the tenant to kill up to a thousand rabbits over a two-year period, though he was not allowed to enter the coverts where they bred. Such agreements possibly existed with the other tenants.

Despite his two marriages, Jervoise died in 1847 at the age of seventy-eight without an heir and the estate came under the management of three trustees. One of them was his sister Mary, who was married to the

George Purefoy Jervoise
(1770–1847) and his first wife,
Elizabeth Hall (1770–1821)

Reverend Francis Ellis, the Rector of Lasham. The latter, after assuming the additional surname and arms of Jervoise, came to inherit the estates at Herriard and at Britford. Jervoise also had a brother, Richard Purefoy, who had died leaving just one daughter and she was married to Thomas Fitzgerald, the owner of Shalstone House in Buckinghamshire. The Fitzgerald family thus succeeded to the estates of Preston and Nutley and, though they did not actually come to reside in the parish till the 1860s, they carried out all the responsibilities their position entailed.

The acquisition of the Hall estates had also brought Jervoise the fine houses of North and South Hall. The latter was usually let to the clergy while North Hall was occupied by a succession of wealthy young gentlemen. Built in 1769, the latter house stood in about two acres of parkland with a walled kitchen garden and some ten acres of pasture on the hill behind. It was thus a highly desirable residence, particularly for say an elder son filling in the time until the day he would inherit his family's country seat.

(Left) Charles Edmund Rumbold, 1788–1857; (Right) Francis Ellis Jervoise, 1809–81

One such occupant in the early 1840s was Jervoise's nephew, Francis Ellis, the son of the Rector of Lasham. He was in his early thirties when he came to North Hall, having married for the second time in 1841 and was to have ten children of whom the first two boys were born at Preston. In addition to the house, his uncle also granted him the shooting rights on Nutley Down, but his parties were not seen there very often as the game proved to be rather sparse. Ellis left North Hall in about 1847, lived for a couple of years at Britford, and then took up residence at Herriard Park. He was very much in the Jervoise mould, serving as J.P. and Deputy-Lieutenant of the County, and in 1852 as High Sheriff, during which year he attended in state the funeral of the Duke of Wellington.

A man of similar background was George Errington. His family dwelt at Lexden Park near Colchester and his father was a J.P., Deputy-Lieutenant, High Steward of Colchester, and in 1860 High Sheriff of

The children of Francis Ellis Jervoise in about 1849. (From left) Selina, Arthur Tristram, John Purefoy and Francis Michael

Essex. Errington's wife came from Bitterne near Southampton and after their marriage in 1852 they dwelt at various houses in the southern part of the county before coming to North Hall in the early 1860s. By then they had five children and kept a staff of six servants. Another occupant of North Hall was Major Samuel Yorke-Martin who came from a Devon family and had begun his military career as an Ensign in 1825. He had progressed quickly by the purchase of commissions, eventually becoming a captain in 1829 in the South Hampshire Regiment. Shortly after he

15

joined, the regiment began a tour of duty which lasted till 1842 and included Gibraltar, Demerara, Berbice, Barbados and Canada, and it was while in the West Indies that he seems to have met his wife, Elizabeth. He retired from the Army on half-pay in 1843 and they lived at various houses in the West Country before coming to North Hall in 1850 where they remained for about two years.

Close to the entrance of North Hall stood another house owned by the Jervoises, known as Preston Cottage, a simple thatched dwelling which was occupied for over twenty years by Miss Harriet Blunt. She kept a cook, maid, and a groom and gardener, and rented some stables in the adjoining property from the village butcher. The Blunts were a Nether Wallop family and Harriet, born in 1785, had been the youngest in a family of six. Her brother Edward became the owner of Kempshott Park while her nephew Walter succeeded in 1832 to the family home of Wallop House and as well as being the local Vicar, served as a J.P. By the 1850s Harriet was aunt to a good number of nephews and nieces, amongst whom the clergy were strongly in evidence. Her nephew James, who married a parson's daughter in 1863, was possibly the most noteworthy for he rose in time to become the Vicar of Old Windsor and also Chaplain to the Queen.

*

The owner of the Preston House estate, Charles Edmund Rumbold, was in quite a different mould from that of the Jervoises, for his family's wealth had been acquired only a few years before. His father, later Sir Thomas Rumbold, had started out in life with few prospects, for the grandfather, a purser aboard an East Indiaman, had been a gambler and spendthrift and had left his family in penury. Thomas entered the service of the East India Company in 1752 at the age of sixteen, sailed for India, and in the succeeding years acquired for himself a substantial fortune. Later, when Governor of Madras, he was also given a baronetcy. Sir Thomas's first wife died in childbed in India and afterwards such a feud developed between himself and their three children that he finally disinherited them all. His second wife bore him one son, Charles Edmund. Born in 1788, the boy was three years old when his father died, but he inherited all the family's property. Sir Thomas's will naturally led to great

16

bitterness between the two branches of the family. Saddled with a baronet-cy but little money, the elder branch of the Rumbolds retired to the continent where they lived in difficult straits for many years until one of them managed to rise high in the Diplomatic Service and thus restore the family fortunes.

Like any son of the nobility, Charles Edmund spent a few years at university and was finally awarded his Master's Degree at Trinity College, Cambridge, in 1814. Four years later at the age of thirty he became M.P. for Great Yarmouth in Norfolk and, apart from two short breaks, he was to represent that Borough for the next thirty-seven years. He was described as a 'moderate whig' who held 'liberal opinions' and was inclined 'to radical reform principles', but in practice his Parliamentary career proved to be undistinguished. This was mainly because his prime interest was in playing the role of the leisured country gentleman, and it was his desire to acquire a country estate which eventually brought Rumbold to Preston House.

Preston House with the West Park beyond

17

The mansion had been built in about 1730 by William Guidott, whose family was of Florentine origin and had prospered in England as a result of services rendered to Edward VI. Guidott, however, became involved in intrigues surrounding the Court of Queen Anne and his family's position rapidly declined. The estate fell heavily into debt and his successor was eventually forced to sell it in 1783 to a London merchant named John Blackburn. The grounds were considerably developed during Blackburn's time: an Italian garden and three terraces were laid out and the slopes above the house, known as the West Park, were planted with clumps of trees. After 1823 he had the field opposite the house landscaped in the same way and called the East Park. When he died in 1824, however, the estate was once again heavily in debt and it was not till 1829 that the Court of Chancery made an order for it to be sold.

The bulk of the estate was acquired by Charles Rumbold. It cost him £34,000, included four farms, and comprised some 900 acres in Preston and Nutley as well as nearly the whole of Bradley parish. In addition to his Hampshire estate he kept a house at Eccleston Square in Westminister. His wife Harriet, who came from a Kent family, was some twenty years his junior and during the 1830s she bore him three sons: Charles James Augustus, Thomas Henry and Henry Edmund. All of them were brought up by tutors, one of whom was a Prussian Doctor of Philosophy named Arnauld Braun, and then in 1854 they were admitted to various colleges at Cambridge.

Rumbold soon added to the ornamental gardens about the house, constructed avaries and increased the acreage of parkland. Two cottages in an old rookery near the Turnpike were demolished and a new sweeping drive laid out, approaching the house from the north-east. On the south side another curving tree-lined drive was established which, being the route the household took on Sunday mornings, became known as the Church Walk. Trees were planted by the hundred during the 1840s, not only in the East and West Park but on the hilltops in the surrounding countryside, and these would eventually give the village a much less open appearance than it had in the 1850s.

The house and grounds were tended by a staff of more than fifteen people. Those living in the house consisted of a lady's maid, cook, three house servants, a headman and gardener. The butler, Thomas Coulson,

The stables at Preston House. The clocktower was acquired by John Blackburn in 1801 from Southampton Town Hall

lived with his family in a cottage just opposite the drive entrance. He had been in service with the Rumbolds all his life and was to be rewarded after his master's death with a pension and the freehold of his cottage. Two other gardeners and the groom also lived in cottages close to the estate while wives of two of the farmworkers worked in the laundry. They were all kept busy, for Rumbold entertained lavishly. He was made a member of the Hampshire Hunt in 1834, kept a pack of harriers and often held shooting parties on the estate. Over the years, however, he became intensely preoccupied with his health and would go every summer to a fashionable watering-place in Germany. For most of the 1850s he seems to have been too ill to take much interest in either the estate or Parliament. He was at Brighton when he died at the end of May 1857.

His widow continued to live at Preston House for another three years before she sold the estate to John-James King, a J.P., Deputy-Lieutenant and a former High Sheriff for Sussex. As for Rumbold's three sons, Thomas Henry went into the legal profession, Henry Edmund joined the Army, and Charles James Augustus just became highly eccentric. Soon after his marriage in 1863, he bought a Georgian mansion at Brighton and

19

lived there in poor health for the rest of his life, almost totally absorbed in obscure religious controversies. Every afternoon he would drive out along the front and give money plus a religious tract to any beggar, prostitute or drunkard he might see. In fact, but for his strong-willed wife, he might easily have given away Sir Thomas Rumbold's entire fortune.

John-James King, Esquire (1794–1867) of Preston House with his gamekeeper and stable boy.

*

The horizons of the landed gentry were far wider than Preston Candover. In matters of local government, their province was at the County level and they rarely concerned themselves directly with village affairs. Nevertheless, they did feel they had certain duties towards their village, especially in the making of donations to local charities. Jervoise's obituary spoke of 'his unobtrusive piety and private charities' whilst of Rumbold it

20

was said that 'he was ever ready, from an accurate sense of Christian responsibility, to aid in any charitable object which might benefit the labouring classes or relieve distress'. He was as equally liberal with his donations in Great Yarmouth but not apparently with the impoverished elder branch of the Rumbolds, several of whom made fruitless appeals to him for support. Whether any rivalry existed in village matters between the two wealthy landowners is difficult to say. The running of the village school, for instance, was dominated by the Jervoises and Fitzgeralds, and so in 1853 Rumbold set up a school at Bradley to be run under his exclusive patronage.

The close ties between gentry and village were most clearly demonstrated when the new church was built at Preston. A list of subscribers published in 1887 is thick with various admirals, generals and other gentlemen of the Purefoy–Jervoise–Fitzgerald family. There were also other people whose families no longer lived in the village but who still felt they had a duty to contribute, like George Errington who donated £2. Miss Blunt had left the village in the late 1850s and died at Odiham in 1867, but her relatives contributed £50 to the new church in her name as well as making a special gift of the pulpit and the marble columns in the east window. John-James King also died in 1867 and his family left the village shortly afterwards, but when approached for a contribution to the church, his eldest son made a gift of the chancel window. Whether any such approach was made to the sons of Charles Rumbold is not known, but certainly the name of Rumbold is noticeably absent from the list.

21

4

The Country Parson

In church matters the 1850s was an important time in Preston and Nutley, for until then both parishes had suffered from long years of neglect. They lay within the Diocese of Winchester and since the sixteenth century their churches had been under the patronage of the Dean and Chapter of Winchester Cathedral. Nutley was at first a separate parish but the living proved too small to support an incumbent, and in about 1650 it became a Chapelry of the Vicarage of Preston Candover. Throughout most of the seventeenth century the incumbency was held by three successive generations of the Waterman family, but after the death of John Waterman in 1725 the Vicarage was attached to a canonry or minor canonry of Winchester Cathedral. From then on the vicar never actually resided in the parish, but left his work in the care of a resident curate.

The man who held the living in 1851 was the Reverend Thomas Westcombe. Born in 1784, he had gained his Master's Degree at Trinity College, Oxford, in 1819 and for some years thereafter ran a small school in Winchester. Then, on becoming a minor canon of the Cathedral in 1826, he had been appointed vicar not only of Preston Candover but also of Letcombe Regis in Berkshire. He also served as Chaplain of Winchester College. His home was located at St Peter's Street in Winchester and, like his predecessors, he left his two parishes in the care of curates.

For his time this was quite a normal state of affairs and perfectly understandable, for the living in one country parish could not possibly maintain a man in his position. The vicar's income was based upon the Tithe, which in Preston and Nutley was divided into two parts. There were firstly the Rectoral Tithes, which were appropriated by the Cathedral and which were commuted in 1839 to a rent of £459. Secondly, there were the Vicarial Tithes, which were appropriated by the vicar and these amounted to £202. The Church also owned glebelands which totalled 40 acres and were valued at £30 per annum. From these sources the vicar derived a total income of about £230 which made it quite a poor living. The upkeep of the church itself was financed partly by a special rate levied at threepence in the pound and also by the rent from an allotment of 11 acres.

The benefice was responsible for two churches, both dedicated to St Mary. One of them was at Nutley village, a small church rebuilt in 1845 and designed by a local architect in the Early English style. It cost £946, the sum being raised by subscriptions, and it could accommodate 160 people. The church at Preston had been built at the end of the seventeenth century, the original church on the site which dated from 1190 having been destroyed by fire. The Guidotts had later added a side-aisle while the Halls erected a gallery for their personal use, but by the 1850s the building was in a bad state. The Rural Dean stated in 1871 that it was incommodious and had no pretence of architecture; the wooden flooring and the pulpit were quite rotten and the walls were spreading. 'Nothing,' he concluded, 'could present a more mean and dilapidated appearance than the present building.' Sumner Wilson was to call it 'an unsightly barn'. Furthermore, the churchyard had become so overcrowded that each time a new grave was dug, the remains of at least one long deceased parishioner would be unavoidably exhumed.

The original vicarage at Nutley had disappeared but the one at Preston remained. Situated next door to the church, it too presented a mean appearance—a plain six-roomed cottage with an old coach-house at the side. Not surprisingly, the clergy let the house to a labourer's family and lived instead at South Hall. There were six curates appointed between 1837 and 1851: Robert Denny, Robert Wedgwood, Stephen Terry, Henry Wickens, Richard Dalton and William Barnard. Most of them were graduates of Oxford Colleges and Preston was usually their first appoint-

23

ment. Their careers would often take them on to very different parts of the country. Robert Denny later became curate at Shedfield near Fareham, Richard Dalton went to Kelmarsh Rectory near Northampton, and Henry Wickens became Curate of Wyken near Coventry where he also

The old St Mary's church at Preston Candover

conducted services in the Chapel of the Duke of Binley. Since they could afford to live in a house like South Hall, it would seem the curates were fairly affluent men. Stephen Terry, for example, the son of a wealthy land-owner at Dummer, was unlikely to have depended solely on his curate's salary of £80 a year.

Another of the curates, Robert Wedgwood, was able to keep a staff of four at South Hall to attend on just himself and his wife. He was a grandson of the famous Staffordshire potter, Josiah Wedgwood. Robert's father, John Wedgwood, broke away from the family firm to embrace banking and horticulture, but had to be saved from bankruptcy by his family who set him up with a small estate near Bath. He had his sons make their careers in the Guards or, in the case of Robert, the Church. Born in 1806, Robert had been educated at Charterhouse and had then graduated from Trinity College, Cambridge, and was to devote most of

The old rectory with the church beyond

his life to being Rector of Dumbleton in Gloucestershire. But for about four years Preston had a member of a large illustrious family as its curate, of whom perhaps the most famous member was to be his cousin, Charles Darwin.

South Hall, built in 1812 for Elizabeth Hall (1733–1818), a sister of Thomas Hall, Lord of the Manor

25

In general the Church in the early years of the nineteenth century was still regarded as a quiet profession, suitable for the sons of gentlemen. It is difficult to tell how much the Curates of Preston actually did. During the 1840s there were about fifteen to twenty baptisms to administer each year at Preston, up to ten funerals and three weddings. A wedding at Nutley church was more of a rarity, but there were usually about five baptisms and a couple of funerals. One thing not expected of the curate was any great religious zeal, for that would have been viewed as unseemly, like the rantings of a Methodist preacher.

It was during these years that the Wesleyans, Primitive Methodists and other Non-Conformist groups found a considerable following in the rural labouring class, much to the concern at first of the gentry and clergy. The number of strict Dissenters in Preston remained small, however—no more than about four families. Between 1840–61 there seem to have been only two families in which none of the children was baptised. The father of one of them was a wood-dealer named David Wyeth, whose sons were called Cale, Amos and Jesse. When he left the village in the early 1860s, a strip of garden beside his cottage became the site of a Primitive Methodist Chapel. Sunday school and services were held there every Sunday, and a camp meeting was held annually by the green.

During the period of Thomas Westcombe's incumbency at Preston, great changes were made in the Established Church. Not only was it a time of great spiritual revival but also administrative reform. Two statutes would have been of particular concern to him: one forbade a vicar to hold more than one living and the other forbade him to be absent from it. It was often some time before these reforms affected the individual parish and Westcombe carried on as before until 1849, when he ceased to be a Minor Canon or Chaplain of the College, and actually came to reside in his parish, though he continued to be the absentee Vicar of Letcombe Regis.

Westcombe's arrival must have been quite an event, for during the twenty-two years since his presentation to the parish, he had administered just three baptisms and two funerals. During 1850, however, he conducted eight baptisms, the same number as his curate. But his arrival had upset all the long-standing arrangements, for the curate now had to make way for him at South Hall and move into the humble rectory cottage.

Westcombe was in his mid-sixties by this time and was to be at Preston for only three years. With his death in July 1852, the plurality he had enjoyed came to an end and the following December Preston and Nutley were presented with a new resident vicar, the Reverend Edward Wickham.

*

Born in January 1801, Edward Wickham was the son of a wealthy Winchester family and became a notable classical scholar at New College, Oxford, where he graduated in 1823. In 1826 he was awarded his Master's Degree and took Holy Orders, and then in 1830 he returned to Winchester to take up a teaching post at Winchester College where his family had many close connections. Edward and his brothers had received their education there. His younger brother, Frederick, became a Commoner Tutor in 1837 and Second Master in 1846. Another brother, William, was at one time the school doctor. Edward himself was appointed Assistant Master in 1830 but he remained for only three years and then left to become Headmaster of a school called Eagle House at Hammersmith, which was described as 'a first rate establishment for the education of young gentlemen'. He was married in 1833 to Christiana St Barbe, a daughter of Charles White, the Rector of Shalden, and a great-niece of Gilbert White, the famous naturalist of Selborne. They were to stay at Eagle House for some fifteen years, during which time they had six children. Christiana died in 1846. In April 1851 Wickham became curate at Frimley in Surrey after its previous curate had been shot by a gang of burgulars. The family were there for eighteen months before he was appointed Vicar of Preston Candover and Nutley.

Wickham would of course have been acquainted with Thomas Westcombe since the latter had been Chaplain at Winchester College, and this may have assisted his appointment. Wickham was just fifty-two by then and married to Louisa Boak, a woman some twenty years his junior. He was soon busy trying to make up for the years of neglect in the parish. Some start had been made on this just before his arrival when £300 was spent on repairs to Preston church. Wickham put more effort into running the school and drew up plans for a new one. He handled all the charities and in 1855 set up a reading room which soon acquired two hundred volumes. The number of services in the church would have been increased

27

at this time to two on Sunday and one in the week, and enriched by such new features as the sermon, hymn singing, the choir, and the harvest festival. The village band and later a harmonium provided the musical accompaniment, for there was no organ until the new church was built some thirty years later.

Like many of the new breed of clergymen, Wickham no doubt had to face a considerable struggle in overcoming the legacy of neglect and corruption in the Established Church. One place where this occurred was the Parish Vestry. The affairs of a parish were handled very informally at this time. A group of people, principally the farmers, would meet at the vestry every Easter and simply share out the official posts between them. In Preston these posts consisted of two Churchwardens, two Overseers who dealt with poor relief, and two Surveyors of the Highways who organised the maintenance of the public roads. Apart from the latter post, each man served for a period of two successive years. In a small parish like Nutley, one farmer served continuously in all three posts.

The year before Wickham was appointed, a surveyor had been engaged at a fee of £42 to carry out a revaluation of the parish. This had become necessary because over the previous thirteen years the rateable values of property in the village had become quite out of date, although the Vestry Minute Book gives no idea as to why such a state of affairs had been allowed to develop. Wickham attended the first vestry meeting of 1853 and took the chair, thus pushing out Farmer Lainson who had been the chairman for several years. This was probably quite a touchy occasion for until then the parish officers had never had the clergy interfering in their affairs. A minute of the next meeting in October 1853 reads:

The Overseers be requested to use the power belonging to their office in enforcing the payment of the rents for the cottages belonging to the parish: it having appeared that certain of them had not been paid for some years.

It would thus seem that certain parish matters were in a muddle and the new vicar saw it as his duty to sort them out.

Wickham had one problem which had not troubled his predecessor and that was the inadequacy of his income. 'Out of the pittance which this Living provides,' he wrote in 1861, 'two thirds are absolutely consumed

28

before I receive anything, and the remainder, after deducting the usual public charities, is considerably less than what I have been obliged to pay to my Curate.' By that time his three sons by his first marriage were at Oxford, while during their time at Preston Louisa had given birth to six children. With a house like South Hall and a staff of six to maintain, he must have had some extra source of income. All this undoubtedly lay behind the circumstances which eventually brought the vicar and his parishioners to the Michaelmas Session Appeals at Winchester in 1860.

The case of Wickham *v.* the Parish of Preston Candover was in itself highly technical, but since the costs involved came to £138, the issue must have been of considerable local importance. Wickham's standpoint seems to have been that, although he could easily have administered his duties on his own, he was required by the Bishop to keep a curate whose annual salary was £80. The living could not support both vicar and curate, and Wickham claimed, therefore, that the income of the combined parishes should be increased. This was opposed by the Parish on the grounds that the only reason for retaining a curate was to administer to the Chapelry of Nutley, and Nutley they claimed was a separate parish. Therefore, the curate's salary should be derived from the income of Nutley alone. The case thus rested on the complex issue of whether the two parishes had ever been legally made into one benefice, and this required the consultation of various ancient documents. The perplexed gentlemen of the Bench finally concluded that they were in fact one benefice and so Wickham won his case.

About the time the appeal was heard, the post of curate changed hands. Henry Prentice, after nearly ten years at Preston, left to become the Rector of Holford in Somerset. His place was taken by Thomas Ridley, a married man in his mid-forties who had been curate of Bullington and Tufton for fourteen years. Though he was to live in Preston for nearly twenty years and sometimes officiated at the church, his actual appointment was to the curacy of Wield. The Bishop's Register sheds no light on the affair at all, but it would seem that no sooner had the appeal been settled than the bishop allowed the vicar to dispense with a curate and so the prime cause of the trouble was removed. The embittered feelings of the parishioners may be imagined and it seems they retaliated at a vestry meeting held less than a month after the appeal. Wickham was not present; Farmer Lunn took the chair and the minute of the meeting reads: 'It was agreed to amend the Rate on the Vicarial Tithes from £59.10.7*d* to £97.11.9*d* ... the Rate to be made at one shilling in the Pound.'

Some indication of the feelings in the parish is given in a letter Wickham wrote a couple of months later. It was intended for a lady who had assisted in the village charities and he clearly wanted to gloss over any problems. 'I regret to find,' he wrote, 'that you imagine we are living in a state of disunion and that anything I have said, should have in any measure confirmed such an idea. I can assure you that if such a state exists, or has existed since I have lived here, it has been entirely without my knowledge.' He did go on to admit, however, that there were 'inconveniences' which arose mainly because the relief of poverty in the parish fell heavily and unequally on just a few people.

The same letter ended on a dismal note concerning the prospects for a new school which Wickham did not consider to be too hopeful. His family circumstances at this time would not have been too happy either. Three years before he and Louisa had lost one of their daughters and in November 1860, during all the troubles in the parish, their son Walter died at the age of sixteen weeks. Wickham himself died a year or so later, one Friday evening in June 1862 at Symonds Street in Winchester, the home of his two spinster sisters. A week later he was buried at Preston, the service being conducted by Godfrey Bolles Lee, the Warden of Winchester College. Louisa also died in the November of that year after giving birth to another child and was buried beside her husband. The child was called Amy and baptised a week later by Wickham's eldest son, Edward Charles, who by then was a tutor and dean of New College. After a distinguished career at Oxford, he was to become Headmaster of Wellington College in Berkshire in 1873 and twenty years later Dean of Lincoln, and was to marry Agnes, the eldest daughter of the famous William Ewart Gladstone.

*

Wickham was succeeded by the Reverend Sumner Wilson, a graduate of Christ Church, Oxford, and a nephew of Bishop Sumner of Winchester. He was thirty-one when appointed, a tall thin man who seemed to walk everywhere at a breathless rate. He certainly set about his work with vigour. Improvements were carried out to the school. The overcrowded graveyard was extended. The old rectory was enlarged, re-roofed with tiles, and transformed into a handsome house. No sooner was it finished than he exchanged part of the glebe for a field further up the village and had a new vicarage built. It was completed in 1873 whereupon the rectory was sold.

The Reverend Sumner Wilson, 1831–1917

Sumner Wilson's main ambition, however, was to have a new church built at Preston. For years he pressurized the Bishop and the Ecclesiastical Commissioners, and once agreement had been reached he wrote to everyone he knew for a subscription. A new site was required more in the centre of the village and a field was finally acquired on the south side of the green. A design was produced by A. W. Blomfield, an eminent architect of many Victorian churches, and work commenced in 1884, the foundation stone being laid by Mrs Purefoy Fitzgerald. All but the chancel of the old church was demolished at the same time to provide flints for the new one. Its four bells were housed in a barn and services had to be held in the schoolroom. The new church cost some £3700 and proved to be a fine building of brick and flint with a tall slim steeple, situated in an ideal setting. It was consecrated one Thursday morning in July 1885 by the bishop, after which about a hundred clergy and friends had lunch on the vicarage lawn. Some 250 parishioners were invited to the vicarage later in the day for tea and then it was back to the new church for an evening service with the archdeacon.

The new St Mary's church at Preston Candover, being made ready for consecration, July 16th 1885

As well as containing the names of the gentry, the list of subscribers to the church included many of the former curates. Henry Wickens gave £20, Richard Dalton and Robert Wedgwood £2 each, William Barnard and Stephen Terry a guinea each. Amongst the special gifts for the interior was the altar desk, donated by Henry Prentice. And then there was the reredos, the ornamental screen behind the altar which depicted two kneeling angels. A small brass plaque was put up in a corner nearby which read: 'In loving and reverential memory of Edward Wickham M.A. Vicar of this Parish 1853–62. The Reredos of the New Church was given by his children.' Clearly whatever 'disunity' might have attended Edward Wickham's incumbency, by 1885 it had long been forgotten.

5

The Village School

One of the clergy's special responsibilities in Preston Candover was the provision of education. Some kind of schooling had existed for many years under the auspices of the local gentry, but it affected only a few of the children. John Blackburn had provided a school at Bradley and another in the grounds of Preston House, but neither was endowed and so they ceased after his death. Another school was created by the Reverend William Oades, the Rector of Dummer, whose family farmed Moundsmere in the seventeenth century. In 1730 he bequeathed a sum of £2.10.0*d* to be expended each year in the teaching of six girls at Preston.

This could have been the origin of a school which was held in the old rectory until about the 1850s. By then the original bequest had been supplemented by subscriptions, mostly from the gentry and clergy, as well as by a fee of twopence a week from each child. In an account of 1840 the total income of the school came to £21 of which £16.16.0*d* comprised the salary of the teacher, Mrs Parker. The exact number who attended the school is not known, though by this time they included both boys and girls. Apart from reading, writing and simple arithmetic, the girls also learnt cooking, brewing, smocking and shirtmaking, but most important of all, straw-plaiting. The latter activity earnt the school a little money, for the finished plaits were taken to Basingstoke for making into hats. As for the boys, they were taught carpentry, farmwork, shoe-mending, bricklaying and gardening, not actually at the rectory itself but by being sent for odd days to the various farms, gardens and workshops. Farmer

Lunn of Manor Farm gave reading lessons on Sunday afternoons to those boys apprenticed to him, his only lesson book being the Bible.

A Dames' School also existed in Preston during the 1850s, run by two spinsters in their forties named Harriet and Mary Clark. Their brother was a carpenter and they lived in a tiny cottage at the side of the timber-yard. Most of the pupils were the infant daughters of the craftsmen and better-off labourers, for whom the main purpose of the Dames' School was to get the children out from under their mother's feet for a few hours each day.

Looking north-east towards the village pond. The Dames' School was held in the small thatched cottage

Both these schools disappeared eventually, leaving just one establishment, the Preston Candover National School. This school had originated in 1772 when Thomas Hall had directed in his will that the net rent and profits arising from a barn, house and eight acres of land should be yearly applied in instructing to read and write as many children of Preston Candover as the yearly profits would allow. The arrangements were later reorganised by George Purefoy Jervoise who, by an Indenture of 1826, decreed that his Manor Farm in Preston should pay £12 a year for the education of ten poor boys, to be nominated with their master by the Lord of the Manor. The endowed school together with the master's house lay near the green, while the land which helped finance it was situated at the rear. As for the running of the school, Jervoise directed that the master 'should use his best endeavours and ability to educate and instruct ten poor boys ... in reading, writing and cyphering (the parents of such children finding books, slates, pens and other articles necessary for their use and for such instruction)'. The master also had to allow 'the said Scholars six weeks holiday in the harvest season and also two weeks from St Thomas' Day in each and every year and shall also be at liberty to give and allow unto the Scholars such other holidays as he should think fit so that the same did not exceed two half-holidays in any one week'.

From such humble beginnings the school gradually increased its intake, from seven boys in 1821 to a total attendance in 1853 of about eighty boys, girls and infants drawn from Preston and Nutley. This meant that just over half of all the children aged between five and thirteen were able to attend, though only eleven of them were over ten years of age. With such an increase in numbers, the original endowed school became quite inadequate and during the 1840s a cottage was lent by the Jervoise and Fitzgerald families for use as a schoolroom. In 1853 the total income for the school came to over £57, of which the Endowment amounted to £12 and the rent of the allotment to one pound. The fees paid by the pupils' parents amounted to one halfpenny a week and in 1853 they produced £7.17.2½d. The remaining £36 was largely subscribed by the gentry.

The main items of expenditure were the salaries of the master and mistress. It is doubtful if the quality of teaching was very high in the early years. In the 1820s the job rested with a labourer's widow, Mrs Goater, whose son James later took over. William Benham, master from about 1836–45, was also drawn from the labouring class and like James Goater he went back in later years to being a farm worker. Benham's successor was William Hodgkins, the first master to be appointed from outside the village. He had been born at Chipping Norton and was in his early forties when he and his wife Emma came to teach at Preston after previous posts at Charlebury near Oxford and at Burghclere. His salary for 1853 was £36 while Emma's was £8.

The house which the Fitzgeralds loaned for use as a schoolroom had been built in 1821 and was used originally as chandler's shop. Constructed of bricks with a tiled roof, it consisted of two rooms: the Big Room, about forty feet by eleven, and an Infants Room, twenty-one feet by eleven. The Big Room had a fireplace at either end, but both rooms were made cold through having brick floors and these were eventually boarded over. The rooms also suffered from poor lighting which was not improved until 1872 when the windows were raised. As for the running of the school, the fuel usually came to about £4 a year, sweeping the chimneys 2/-, and the books, stationery and sundries a little less than £2.

The school as it looked in about 1900. *The original house comprised the section on the right.*

The school was managed during the 1850s by six trustees who included the vicar and the two churchwardens. Their efforts seem to have been directed not only to running the existing school but also to having a completely new one built on the site of the original endowed school building and master's house. The cost was estimated at £500, for which the trustees requested financial assistance in 1859 from the Lords of the Committee of Council on Education. The plans, however, failed to materialise, most probably because the number of pupils had been diminishing during the 1850s in line with a general decline in the population as a whole—from eighty pupils in 1853 to fifty-five in 1862, and this made the task more manageable. Instead of a new school, therefore, the house loaned by the Fitzgeralds was made into a permanent schoolroom, and a year after Sumner Wilson's appointment a plan was drawn up to erect a master's house at one end of it. The Fitzgeralds agreed to pay for this work in return for the occupation of the school land. The old endowed school and house were made into cottages and let, their income being added to the existing endowment.

The reduction in the size of classes meant that the job could now be done by one person with the aid of a pupil teacher. The last married couple to be appointed, Mr and Mrs Fencott, were replaced in about 1860 by one schoolmistress, Miss Elizabeth Hathouse. The old schoolhouse being in need of repairs, she lodged with the family of the village tailor. The quality of the teacher had progressed considerably. Miss Emma Meaden, appointed in April 1863, was twenty-two years old and had received her teaching certificate in 1861 at the Bristol and Gloucester Diocesan Training School. She had been engaged under inspection for about three years at a school in Durley near Bishops Waltham, after which she had come to Preston. Her annual salary was £30 while her assistant was paid a pound.

The work of successive schoolmistresses was to be very much overshadowed by the presence of Sumner Wilson. He not only gave scripture lessons three times a week but other lessons as well—dictation, reading, spelling and arithmetic—and sometimes he examined the whole school in three or more subjects. There was no attendance officer appointed till 1883 so he took this duty upon himself, calling on the parents concerned to find out why their children were not at school. According to the log book, which began in 1863, he was occasionally given some frank excuses: the children had gone to the races or to a cricket match, a funeral or a club feast. After harvest many of the absentees would be out leazing, nutting or blackberrying. The most common excuse for absence, however, was lack of footwear.

The vicar's wife was also a regular visitor to the school and took singing lessons once a week. Then there were visits from the gentry, particularly the Fitzgeralds who continued to be the chief patrons. When Colonel and Mrs Purefoy Fitzgerald came to live at North Hall in November 1866, the children were given a half-holiday. The couple became regular visitors; the Colonel sometimes taught a class while his wife took great interest in the needlework. When the weather was bad the children who brought their dinners were invited to North Hall for hot soup. The daughters of the Fitzgerald and Wilson families would visit the school too, so that sometimes there could be five or six visitors in one week. Occasionally Mrs Wilson brought sweets with her, and at Christmas a party would be provided at which Sumner Wilson would distribute cloaks and smocks as presents and give away books as prizes for good conduct. And of course, like every other Victorian school in the country, Preston Candover had to have its school photograph, introduced in the 1870s and repeated thereafter in each successive year in the same unchanging format.

The staff and pupils of Preston Candover School in 1897. The Headmistress, Miss Street, is on the left; her assistants at the back. Centre row, fourth from right, is Daisy Thorp, the butcher's daughter, later Mrs D. D. Cosier. She became Headmistress in 1909 at the age of twenty-three and remained until her retirement in 1952

6

The Tradesmen

In 1840 the Parish Officers of Preston Candover decided that two cottages should be built near Axford to house some of the poorer families in the village. The project was to be very much a local undertaking. Farmer Lunn provided lime, bricks and straw, and Thomas Heath, the Bailiff of Preston Farm, supplied poles, rods and laths. The bricklaying was done by the village builder William Smeeth, the carpenter Jonas Clark did the woodwork and fixed the laths, while John Whitear the blacksmith made the ironwork. Such craftsmen were very important to village life at this time and with the shopkeepers and other tradesmen they made up a distinct and colourful class of people.

The village of Preston Candover had three shops in 1851: the Thorps' butcher's business, the Vines' grocer's shop, and the Allens' grocer's shop and bakehouse. There was a malthouse run by Martin Thorp while James Thorp was publican of the New Inn, a low thatched building by the green. There was also a beershop at the Forge Cottage. At Axford there was another beershop in the home of Old Widow Waight and a grocer's shop on Axford Hill at the home of William Thorp the wheelwright. There were also such people as the wood dealer, David Wyeth, and a contractor named William Ellis who set up in business in the mid-1850s, taking his steam traction engine and threshing tackle round to the various farms.

The running of such trades was very much a family affair. Charles Mercer, a grocer, baker and draper and a dealer in hardware, hops and coal, came to Preston in the 1850s from Basingstoke and ran his business

40

Looking south down the village street with the pond in the distance. The Vines' grocer's shop is on the left; Daniel Light's workshop was at the rear. The house beyond was occupied by the families of William Major, Daniel Wigg, William Self and Jeremiah Chamberlain. On the right is part of the house occupied by John Thorp Junior; his father, along with Alfred and Sydney Thorp, lived in the house beyond

with the help of his wife and brother. James Vine, a Leicestershire man, had previously been a policeman, but he appears to have retired from the Constabulary after his marriage in the mid-1840s and came to live in Preston where he ran a carrier's business while his wife Sabina looked after the shop. The families of other tradesmen, however, had been established for longer, especially the Thorps whose forebears had lived in Preston for over three hundred years. In the early 1800s there had been several branches of the family still living in the area, but by the 1850s they had mostly died out or moved away. One had become a farmer at South Warnborough, another a gamekeeper at Herriard, while a third was a miller at Old Alresford. Those Thorps left in the village belonged to three main stems of the family tree and most were engaged in some sort of business, the most notable being John Thorp the butcher.

41

The house and butcher's shop of John Thorp Junior

Born in 1788, John Thorp had once been the tenant of Manor Farm in Preston, but at the age of twenty-five he decided to give up farming except as a sideline and become a butcher instead. He was a large man of twenty-eight stone, his hair completely white as a result of rheumatic fever. At the time of the enclosure he was the owner of two large houses plus the butcher's shop, and the malthouse, stables and cottage near North Hall. There were some paddocks attached to these properties and he received allotments totalling about seven acres in 1823. On one of them he had two cottages built, one of which he sold to William Smeeth's father who did the building, the other he let to labouring families.

John Thorp was a man of some status in the village, though by 1851, being a widower of sixty-three, he was content to share out his business and property between his sons. His wife Harriet had borne him seven children, of whom only the eldest, George, had left the village to become a farmer and maltster at Cliddesden. John Thorp junior took over the butcher's business, Martin became the maltster, and Sidney worked as a butcher and then tried several enterprises, including a grocer's shop and bakehouse attached to Little Axford Farm. Alfred was the oddest of all the Thorp sons, growing up into an eccentric bachelor. He was a butcher and farmer by trade, tall like his father, and of slow and deliberate speech; he could quote whole sections of the Bible by heart. Most of his leisure time was spent going to funerals at any church for miles around. He kept donkeys in a half-starved condition in the top half of a meadow behind his house, simply because the Lord had ridden on one into Jerusalem. In the lower half of the meadow he would build a hay-rick each year, the hay coming from the Church land which he rented, and he would reckon to sell it for about £100. This money he invested in buying up cottages to let, with such success that on his death in 1879 at the age of fifty-seven, he was worth £1,300, though he died in semi-starvation.

John Thorp Junior (1814–68) and his wife Mary in about 1846

Several other men in the tradesmen class invested their money in small properties. Although the bulk of Preston and Nutley was owned by two gentlemen, the ownership of the cottages and meadows in the village was very complicated. A number of properties were owned by men who didn't actually dwell in the parish. Oxells Farm, for instance, a smallholding on the road to Axford, was held on a lease from Winchester College by one George Lamb. He was an attorney who lived at Worting and among his numerous posts he served as Clerk to the Bench of the Basingstoke Division, the Basingstoke Board of Guardians, and certain Turnpike Trusts. He was also a banker and an agent for several landowners in the district, and had himself bought more than 700 acres in various parishes, sometimes in partnership with other gentlemen. Thus Oxells Farm was one small investment.

The blacksmith shoeing at Axford Farm

Of the local tradesmen who invested in property, the most notable was George Allen. He too belonged to a long established Preston family, though as with the Thorps there were only a few branches left in the village by 1851 and they tended to be George's poor relations. Born in 1806, George was the only surviving son of Joey Allen, the former village carrier. George made his first acquisition in 1834, a meadow and cottage at the top end of the village and then in 1842 he bought a second property for £270 near Manor Farm; a cottage and three-acre field called Shepherd's Close. In 1849 he bought a shop and farm in the centre of the village from a Reverend Dinley for £775, and this served as the Allens' home for the next fifty years. George had modest sums invested in Government stock on which he drew, for example, when purchasing the Reverend Dinley's premises: '1849 Tues May 8th,' he wrote in his diary, 'sold £760 stock for £692 and with dividends then due made £700 paid to Basingstoke Banking House in London ready to receive at Basingstoke'.

The Allens thus acquired some standing in the village which apparently made them rivals in local affairs of the Thorps; both families had their place at the Vestry. Though married three times, George had only one son, born in 1854 and named George Gardiner Allen, and he was able to have him educated not at the village school but at a private boarding school at Stratton. And when George Allen died in 1886, he was given a memorial in one of the smaller windows of the new church—a rare distinction amongst all the other dedications to the gentry and clergy.

*

The craftsmen found in Preston in 1851 included a carpenter and wheelwright, seed-drill maker, blacksmith, boot and shoe maker, bricklayer and tailor. Another blacksmith lived at Axford, a wheelwright on Axford Hill, and a shoemaker just beyond Nutley village. On the hill above Preston Manor Farm lay a small clay pit and kiln, for the high ground in the area was capped by a layer of clay suitable for brick making. The kiln was owned by the Fitzgeralds and run by Thomas Bartlett whose family lived in a cottage at the yard. Another lad worked there too in 1851: Albert Nott from Cookham in Berkshire who made jars for jam, pickles and wine. Then occasionally young journeymen would come and lodge in the village; in 1851 they included a blacksmith from Thruxton and a bricklayer from Alresford.

The craftsmen's business too was very much a family concern and a few of them had been long established, such as the blacksmith, John Whitear, and Stephen and Jonathan Clark, the carpenters. But in most other cases the family were relative newcomers to Preston, moving from another part of the locality when a particular business fell vacant. William Smeeth had been born in Ropley, Thomas Bartlett in Basing, and Moses Giles, the Axford blacksmith, at Wick near Christchurch. William Major the tailor had been born in 1790 at Froyle. In 1816 he had married Ann Ifould, the daughter of a grocer and farmer in Preston, and had started his tailoring business in a cottage at Axford. After Ann's father died in 1819, William moved into a house in the village which the Ifoulds had owned, and let the cottage at Axford to three labourers' families.

William and Ann Major had seven children, five of them sons, and only

45

one of them struck out in a different trade, that of blacksmith. A small village could only support a few people in any one craft and so the sons often had to seek their living elsewhere. George Major became a journeyman tailor based in 1851 at a shop in Wote Street, Basingstoke, but within ten years he had moved round to Church Street and was now a master tailor and draper. His father still had a fair sized business in Preston in the early 1860s, assisted by two married sons, John and Albert. William not only had a son in Basingstoke but also a relative in the tailoring trade in Winchester, so it is possible that he was producing goods for a wider market than just Preston Candover.

Sons followed their father's trade in other families too, like George Smeeth who in 1851 was a journeyman bricklayer in Winchester. The Clark family consisted of two main branches, headed by Jonathan and Stephen, the latter owning the yard and sawpit next to the New Inn. Their sons became carpenters too, though they left the village until their respective fathers were dead and they could inherit the business. Jonathan Clark's son, Jonah, had married a girl from Bentworth and during the 1830s they dwelt at Worthing, returning to Preston in 1845. Likewise, when Stephen Clark died in 1842 the premises were taken over by his eldest son William, who had previously been living in localities as far apart as Jersey and Chelsea.

Several of Preston's craftsmen dabbled in other enterprises. William Major was also the village postmaster and insurance agent. John Whitear also kept a smallholding and his wife Rachel ran the beershop. Then there was Daniel Lazarus Light; born at Dummer in 1819, he had come to Preston in about 1840, a stout thick-set man who wore spectacles and spoke in an affected stilted manner. By trade he was a boot and shoe maker, and in 1844 he bought one half of a property in the village for £300 where he set up his workshop and ran it with the help of an apprentice and a man named Jeremiah Chamberlain. Daniel himself did little shoemaking, however, for he was also a land measurer and for many years worked in the Grange Estate Office at Northington, riding there each day on a pony. He was Secretary of the local Benevolent Society and had many hobbies, including astronomy for which he eventually acquired a telescope and soon had nearly the whole village queuing up at his gate, eager for a quick look through it.

(Left) William Hughes, the sawyer. Born in 1824, he worked as his father had done at Clark's timber-yard in the saw-pit, and lived in one half of the cottage on the opposite side of the road. He married Eliza Whatmore whose family lived next door in 1846. (Right) Daniel Light, the shoemaker

The craftsmen and tradesmen saw themselves as a cut above the class of agricultural labourers. Thus, although some of their daughters helped out as shop assistants or dressmakers, others were found good posts outside the village, not only in service but in other types of work too, like

Elizabeth Smeeth who became an infant teacher at Winchester. Marriages took place only between families in the tradesmen class or with those of the farmers. The family of John Thorp senior was related to the Clarks, the Allens, and to the farmers Lunn and Gardiner. Albert Major's wife was the daughter of a Winchester pipe-maker, while George Clark married a daughter of James Thorp the publican. And as for the widows and the spinster daughters, they could look forward to a modest security in their old age, becoming fundholders like Harriet and Mary Clark or Catherine Thorp, the publican's sister.

Despite appearances, however, several families must have lived close to poverty. The labouring class in the 1850s contained several people who a generation before had followed some kind of trade, like John Adams, a widowed pauper of seventy-two, who in 1823 had been a blacksmith. William Self's father had been a butcher, but William now only carried on the trade in a small way; he was the man each householder called in to kill and cure the family pig. And then there was Henry Ifould, the son of the former grocer and farmer and brother of Ann Major. Henry had taken over the family business in 1819, but in 1838 he became a labourer and by 1851 his family were living as lodgers with Thomas Thorp, a wheelwright's son whose fortunes had not fared too well either. In that year Henry was employed repairing the public roads at a shilling a day, a job only the near destitute would take.

Henry Ifould would clearly have become a poor relation to his sister's family, though it would seem that the Majors too had their difficulties. In 1863 William sold the freehold of his house to a carpenter at Brown Candover and the family went on living there as tenants. William outlived his sons John and Albert, but it would not seem he was able to give much help to John's widow, for in 1865 Sumner Wilson was busy organising a fund for her support. Mr Francis Jervoise of Herriard Park wrote to the Vicar in May, informing him that his family would be pleased to contribute £9 which he felt would enable 'the widow to recommence a small business on her own account if that is thought to be the best thing for the support of herself and the three children'. The fund must have been of great benefit, for Sarah Major carried on as the village postmistress and draper for more than twenty years.

The carrier's wagon outside the Crown Inn on Axford Hill in 1875. The men in the foreground are (from left) George and Harry Giles, John Meachem, Robert Bear the landlord, and Tom Jones the carrier. In 1851 the premises were used as a grocer's shop. The Jones family were carriers at Brown Candover, whilst the two Giles' brothers were the sons of the Axford blacksmith, Moses Giles. John Meachem was a labourer in 1851 living at the top end of Preston village, but he later became bailiff to Mr Young at the Down Farm.

7

The Farmers

For the farmers of Preston and Nutley the month of March 1851 was the wettest most of them could remember. The harvests of the last few summers had been poor and 1851 promised to be no better, with the rain retarding the spring tillage and damp affecting the wheats in both the stack and the granary. Prices were low too; at Basingstoke market wheat had only been fetching up to 45/- a quarter, barley 27/- and oats 21/-. Potatoes, however, had done quite well and the lambing season was proceeding very favourably. In fact, the harvest of 1851 proved to be a good one and ushered in a period of unprecedented farming prosperity.

The bulk of the farmland in the two parishes was now divided up between some eight large farms. At the turn of the century there had been far more but in the ensuing years many had failed because of economic pressures. Several elderly men in the labouring class in the 1850s had once worked their own farms, like William Dallman who was a brother-in-law of John Thorp senior and Stephen Clark, and ended his days as a lodger of his nephew, Alfred Thorp. The Croft, the home of the Gardiner family, was one small farm which managed to survive. Old William Gardiner had held service there under both the Halls and Jervoises, and his land comprised some 53 acres, most of it situated along the Wield Road about a mile from the farmyard beside the green. The farm was carried on after his death in 1860 by his son, Young Will, until he too died in 1879, after which the land was absorbed into The Down Farm. The smallest holding of all was called Little Axford Farm, just 13 acres in extent. A succession of men farmed it in the '40s and '50s, but during the tenancy of Sidney Thorp a fire broke out one night in a barn. His brother Alfred had lent him a ladder and, on hearing about the fire, he hurried up to Axford, found the ladder and pushed it for safe keeping down the well. Consequently no-one could then draw any water and the entire farm was destroyed, never to be rebuilt.

George Allen, however, and later his son, managed to make a living at their smallholding till the early 1900s. The farm which he bought from the Reverend Dinley in 1849 had very little land actually with it but George, like his predecessors, was able to build up a fair acreage by renting fields from other people, especially the vicar, churchwardens and trustees of the school. He also came to rent Oxells Farm and so by 1851 he held a total of 40 acres in various parts of the village. His farming methods were recorded in his diary, as in 1832 when he started renting Shepherd's Close at £4.10.0*d* per annum. The first year he 'sowd with boiling pease, fallowed in winter, sowd and lightly plowd in ground 7 sacks. Next year wheat growd 92 sacks.' About the same time he began farming a field opposite the school called Foots Mead, in which he planted potatoes which 'growd 165 bushels. Next year barley growd little more than 6 sacks.' In succeeding years he left the field fallow and then grew firstly clover on which he turned his sheep, then wheat, barley and white oats.

Lower Farm with the Manor Farmhouse in the distance

The large farms were run rather differently. Only Lower Farm was held by a true Yeoman, William Lainson's family having bought it when the Blackburn estates were sold. Upper Farm (later replaced by Preston

Farm) had been occupied by a tenant during Blackburn's time, but Charles Rumbold managed it himself with the aid of a Bailiff until October 1851 when, probably because of ill-health, he let it to a tenant, Edward Cobden. All the other farms appear to have been held on annual tenancies. Long leases like those granted by Winchester College were rare in the district. The prejudicial effects of annual tenancies were well known, but there was still considerable competition for farms in the area, and a farm which fell vacant could have up to twenty applications within a week.

Several of the farmers remained at their farms throughout the '40s and '50s. None of them came from a family long established in the parish, though nearly all had been born within about ten miles of Preston. The economy of their farms revolved around sheep, each farm having a flock of about five hundred. The most common breed was the Hampshire Downs, though it had recently been improved by crossing with Berkshires and Cotswolds. The flocks were folded on crops of rape, turnips and swedes, and also fed increasingly with oil-cake. Other crops grown included barley, oats, wheat and sainfoin, whilst the remaining livestock consisted of a few milch cows, pigs and poultry, and large numbers of horses—Preston Farm had sixteen, Manor Farm nine along with about four ponies for the personal use of Farmer Lunn and his family. There was little permanent pasture in the valley; just the odd accommodation meadow close to the farmyard. Up on Preston Down there was still some rough pasture and patches of furze, but by 1851 its area had shrunk rapidly. At the Enclosure the Down had totalled 587 acres; by 1838 only 14 per cent had been ploughed up but in the next few years this figure increased to 85 per cent. Much of Nutley Down appears to have been ploughed up at this time too, except for one piece on top of a ridge which was planted with trees.

It was also a time when many hedges were grubbed out and ancient boundaries straightened, so as to make for the efficient use of the new implements being produced by such local manufacturers as Taskers of Andover and Wallis and Stevens of Basingstoke. When the tenant of the Down Farm, John Posnett, died suddenly in September 1860, the implements and machinery on his 350-acre farm consisted of three wagons, two dung carts, four Howard's iron ploughs, three sets of iron Bedford harrows, a three-horse iron-ring roller, a three-wheel land presser, a Garrett's winnowing machine, and a Bennetts' sowing machine. Preston Manor Farm possessed a two-horsepower threshing machine, but most of the farms would probably have hired a contractor like William Ellis, rather than have their own machines. Despite these innovations, most of the farmyards remained largely unaltered, although new yards were constructed at Axford Farm during the 1830s and at the Down and Preston Farms in the early 1840s.

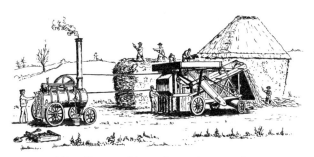

Threshing machine using a steam-engine

The folding of the sheep required large numbers of hurdles, which were derived from the hazel woods above the valley. Every Autumn notices would appear in the *Hampshire Chronicle* such as the following:

Mr Paice will SELL by AUCTION on Tuesday 27th October 1846 at four o'clock in the afternoon at the New Inn, Preston Candover, in lots—15 acres of good underwood in Nutley Wood (South Side) and 4 acres of ditto in Preston Coppice.

The woodmen in the district would go and view the underwood, make their bids and then have about six months to cut and take the timber away. One such man was Richard Merrit who lived at Gobleyhole.

Folding the sheep helped to replenish the soil's fertility, for other animal dung was scarce and various artificial fertilizers often had to be used, such as crushed bones, guano and ashes. Another fertilizer was the chalk, dug from pits in the hedgerows during winter and spread over the fields for the frost to break up into a fine dust. George Allen wrote that in the latter part of November 1835 he put twenty-four cart loads of chalk on Foots Mead, followed by a light coat of dung. Such chalking was especially important on the higher slopes of the valley where the soil tended to be a wet sour clay. In Preston this type of soil was found mainly near Moundsmere and above Manor Farm, but it was more widespread in Nutley where the dells would often reach a considerable depth.

Not all the farmers of course were likely to have been at the forefront of new methods and nor were they equally successful. Charles Smith was the first tenant of the new Down Farm in 1840 and remained there until January 1844. In 1848, while living in Basingstoke, he was ill for a short time and so destitute that he had to apply for poor relief to Preston Parish. He was still living in the town in 1851, employed as a labourer. But he seems to have been the only local farmer in the '40s and '50s who did fail. The others must have been respected figures in the local farming circle. At home their houses were large and simple, though becoming increasingly furnished with finer goods and furniture. They each kept one or two house servants, and John Mountford at Axford, whose wife was to give birth to more than eleven children, also kept a nurse.

Most of the large farms also had about five farm servants, hired on a yearly basis. There were thirty of them in 1851, their ages ranging from thirteen to thirty with a widower of fifty-three kept at Preston Manor Farm. About half came from families living in Preston or Nutley. Most of the servants from other parishes would have been obtained from the autumn hiring fair in one of the local market towns, most probably from the fair at Basingstoke. These boys would usually be farm servants for about three years, during which time they would reckon to learn their craft thoroughly. Those who continued until their thirties often became shepherds or carters. Once he married, however, the servant had to leave the farmhouse, find his own cottage and become an ordinary labourer.

The eight large farms employed about eighty labourers in addition to the thirty servants. This left some sixty men in the two parishes who formed a pool of casual labour on which the farmer could draw along with all the wives, daughters and younger children when he needed extra hands at harvest time or for weeding and lifting rootcrops. An ordinary labourer

54

was hired by the day or the week and earnt about 10/- a week, while a shepherd and carter earnt 11/-. There were also various kinds of bonus: a lump sum of 2/- for harvest work, a penny extra for every new lamb, an extra shilling for making a journey beyond the bounds of the farm. As for the wives and grown-up daughters, they would receive about 4/- a week.

Most of the farmhands lived in the village and only a few shepherds lived out on the down. One isolated shepherd's cottage was called Upper Barn, built in the 1840s and cheaply constructed using walls of chalk rubble held in place by a facing of plaster. It belonged to Preston Farm, while another cottage built after the Enclosure on Preston Down belonged to Lower Farm and became known as Cannon Down Cottages after the Cannons family who lived there throughout the '40s and '50s. Elsewhere in the valley the shepherds lived when necessary in a small 'caravan' close to the flock.

Sheep shearing in the field below the cottage along the Wield Road, occupied by the families of William Smeeth and Richard Allen

The farmers were an important and stable feature of social life in the village and together they dominated the vestry. They contributed to several charities and each donated about 10/- to the school each year. They were particularly careful with their money, however, for the fate of Charles Smith could happen to any one of them. Their expenses quickly built up. Nutley Manor Farm, for instance, consisted of 755 acres and in 1845 the tenant, William Blatch, could reckon to pay £370 a year in rent and £130 in Tithes. Direct taxation, including rates for the poor, the county, the church, highways, as well as income tax, would come to about £110. Despite his arrangements with the Jervoises, Blatch claimed that the damage caused by game led to losses of up to £200 a year. Thus the farmers were quick to rise at further burdens, even if it meant taking their vicar to court.

William Blatch's claims about the damage caused by game made him a figure of some controversy in the district. Besides being a farmer, he was also a valuer of land, stock and growing crops, and this work took him to many parts of Hampshire, Berkshire and Wiltshire. But his estimates of the damage caused by game were often considered extravagant by landowners and their agents. He had been born in 1793 and had worked as a young man with his father at Farleigh Manor Farm, where they lost so much money through rabbits and hares that in 1810 Blatch secretly hired a poacher to help reduce the numbers. He took up the tenancy of Nutley Manor Farm in 1817 and in January 1844 he encouraged a labourer, William Martin, to appeal against a conviction for poaching. The case had arisen when Charles Rumbold was out with his pack of harriers on Nutley Down. The dogs had flushed out a hare which William shot and quickly carried off, but he had been spotted by the gamekeeper and was soon brought before the magistrates. The appeal was taken to the Easter Sessions at Winchester where the conviction was eventually affirmed with £20 costs. Unfortunately the magistrates had allowed William to be released on bail, and once the appeal failed he promptly absconded and for some years eluded all attempts to find him.

As a farmer Blatch was not an easy man to work for. He twice appeared before the magistrates for beating ploughboys; the second time in 1835 he was convicted and fined 2/6d with 5/- costs. In 1838 he and his son were both convicted of asaulting Elizabeth Lynch, the wife of a farmhand, and fined 10/- with £1.4.0d in costs. In 1840 he was taken before the Bench for using his riding whip on Rachel Goodyear's daughter, because she had let some sheep she was watching stray into a field of standing wheat. That time he was fined 2/-. Such assaults were unlikely to have been isolated incidents. Considering this was the man who served as Nutley's Churchwarden and Overseer and its representative on the Board of Guardians, there can have been few labourers who grieved when he gave up the Manor Farm in 1847. He died at Andover two years later and was brought back to Nutley to be buried.

Like the tradesmen, the social position of the farmers was reflected in their marriages with the families of other farmers or the shopkeepers. Some men married soon after taking up their farms. Edward Read was a widower of thirty-five when he arrived at Nutley Manor Farm in 1847 and in November 1849 he married Mary Anne Snuggs, the sister of Charles Rumbold's Bailiff. John Mountford took up Axford Farm in 1842 and a year later he married Mary, the daughter of John Lunn of Preston Manor Farm. The Lunns came to Preston from Old Basing in 1813 and were to be closely linked to several families in the parish. Mary's younger sister Eliza married Martin Thorp in 1848. The eldest son John remained at home assisting his father till he was in his early thirties. Then, on one Sunday in January 1842 he tore a blank page from a ledger, took up his pen and set down his feelings towards Harriet Thorp, the butcher's daughter:

My Dear Friend,

After Much Consideration I address you on a Matter of Great Importance, and should it Prove one that in every way meets your approbation will add much to my comfort, and when I tell you it is your own Dear Self is the Object on which my thoughts and affections are fixed and the one I have Chosen to Share with me the Cares and Pleasures of this Life am sure you will not consider I am acting Imprudently by making it known to you. Now my Dear Friend as this is a matter not to be taken in Hand Lightly I should wish to act towards you and your family uprightly so as to make everything Pleasant and agreeable to All as God forbid I should ever be the means of destroying the Happiness of any Part of a Family. . . I must ask the Favour of a Line from you to give your candid sentiments on the Matter, as it will much relieve the mind of one who is anxious for your welfare. I will now leave it in the Hands of him who doeth all things well and in Conclusion will earnestly hope that ere long we shall be better acquainted and often meet to talk over each other's secrets with Pleasure. If not Permitted to enjoy that privilege I will not murmur but regard it as one of the Greatest of the many Disappointments this world abounds with.

I remain whether Fortunate or unfortunate,
Your Affectionate Friend & Well Wisher,
JOHN LUNN

He was thirty-one at the time he wrote, and Harriet was twenty-three. She apparently received his overture favourably and a courtship began that was to last six years. During this time John took up the tenancy of The Down Farm and finally brought Harriet to live there in July 1848. When his father died in 1854, he gave up The Down Farm and moved back to his old home as the new tenant.

The house at Manor Farm, Preston Candover, the home of the Lunn family

Each year he gave a Harvest Supper at the farmhouse. One of the labourers who worked for the Lunns as man and boy was Moses Mills, and in later years he was to recount how at one supper Tom Martin, the carter, stood up to make a very obsequious speech. Moses, who considered Tom to be 'the laziest son of a bitch he'd ever known', stood up and roundly said so. At that, Tom's fist came up and took the skin off Moses' nose. John Lunn, not always of a tender disposition, sacked them both on the spot, but Moses soon went back and was to serve successive tenants of Manor Farm during the many downturns in farming prosperity over the next sixty years.

Harvest time on Tulls Hill, looking south-east over Lower Farm towards the Preston and Chilton Downs

8

The Labouring Class

Sarah Bulpitt and her family must have been hard pressed in 1851. She had married James Bulpitt in 1824 and thereafter they had lived in a cottage up the Wield Road where she gave birth to nine children. After James died in July 1849 Sarah took any work that was available to make ends meet. In the December of that year, for instance, she had plodded round the fields of Moundsmere, gathering up stones for the roadmenders which earnt her 10/-. By census night in 1851 only the eldest daughter Elizabeth and the three youngest boys were still living at home. Young James was a servant at Axford Farm, George at the Down Farm, and Tony lodging with the Thorns at the Old Marshes Farmhouse. The eldest son Charles was a farmhand lodging at the Shoe Inn at Exton, while Julia, thirteen years old, was in service to Canon Thomas Woodruff at the Cathedral Close, Winchester.

By the 1850s a labouring family like the Bulpitts had been reduced to a level of subservience and poverty at least as bad as at any time in the past. In the '20s and '30s conditions became so harsh that throughout Southern England there were many outbreaks of violence. With no proper police force in country districts, each parish had to look after itself and one method tried in Preston Candover was to form an Association of the farmers, shopkeepers and craftsmen, which would see that felons were brought to justice. In February 1823 handbills were published in the village announcing that:

Whereas several Felonies & Depredations have lately been committed in this Parish, We, the undersigned, do hereby bind outselves to give any person or persons who in future shall give information of the Offender or Offenders, so that they may be brought to Justice, on their conviction, the following Rewards. . . .

The reward depended on the nature of the offence: £10 in the case of breaking into a dwelling house, barn or granary, or setting fire to any building, corn or hay; and also for stealing or maiming any horse, cow or sheep. Smaller rewards were given in cases of theft of other livestock, implements or crops. The occurrence of incendiary fires in the district led Charles Rumbold to maintain a fire-engine at Preston House. When on November 20th 1837 someone set fire to the rectory barns at Dummer, Rumbold, his servants and farmhands rushed over with the engine and apparently saved the day.

With the rising prosperity in farming during the 1850s the countryside became quite settled, but life remained grim for the labouring class. In rural England at this time a married couple with three children could reckon to spend about £20 a year on food, £3 on rent and £8 on clothing. Thus the farm labourer's wage of 10/- a week could just about cover his cost of living. And even if his wife or one of his grown-up daughters was to work in the fields all day, she could never earn more than 4/- a week.

The labouring poor in Preston and Nutley amounted to 432 people in 1851 and they were divided between about a hundred households. Contrary to what the upper classes often imagined, they were far from being a featureless mass of people. The individual families, for instance, were often closely related to each other and thus particular surnames would recur frequently—Alexander, Mills, Kimber, Lynch, Duffin, Wigg, Hopkins, Meachem, Hutton, Thorn, Westbrook and Goodyear. Amongst them were new households like the Bulpitts where the husband came from another parish; men like Henry Large, William Bramley, John Greenaway and William Stratton. And as new families became established, so others diminished—the Adams, Olivers, Knights and Merrits.

Thus most of the large families present in 1851 were the progeny of one couple who had settled in the parish during the previous sixty years or so, and were sometimes still alive in 1851, like William and Ann Mills, born in

61

Whitchurch and Hook respectively, who must have come to Preston in about 1820. Daniel and Sarah Lynch had previously been living at Poole before coming to Preston in about 1780. The various branches of the Alexander family were the offspring of two brothers, Joseph and James, who came from Bradley and who each married Preston girls in the early 1800s. The story of the Wigg family began in 1780 with the marriage of William Wigg to Mary Clee. Mary was from a Preston family but William appears to have been living at Ellisfield. They had three boys and five girls, several of whom married and remained in the parish, as did their grandchildren. Thus by 1851 little Elizabeth Wigg, four years old on census night, had the following relatives living within Preston and Nutley: her widowed mother, three sisters, one brother, both grandparents on her father's side, just the grandfather on her mother's, four aunts, six uncles, three great-uncles, two great-aunts, six second cousins and eighteen first cousins.

Jimmie and Eli Meachem, brothers of John Meachem. Their family home was at Bermondspit, but by 1851 Jimmie, then twenty-six, was a farm servant at Moundsmere. Eli, then twenty-nine, was a gardener, living in a small cottage on Tulls Hill with his wife Harriet and their three young girls, plus his mother-in-law, a nephew and two lodgers

The Labouring Class

By this time the middle classes in Victorian society had become very rigid over such matters as respectability but amongst the labouring poor a more tolerant attitude prevailed. Illegitimacy, for instance, had long been a feature of country life and was not greatly regarded. Of the 343 children in labouring families baptised in Preston and Nutley between 1840–61, eighteen had been born to unmarried mothers. In most of these cases neither mother nor child seems to have been ostracised in the traditional manner. Ten households in 1851 contained an illegitimate child and in six of these the child was living with its grandparents while the mother was away. In two other households the mother had married shortly after the birth and so the child was treated as a stepson or daughter, though retaining the mother's maiden name. Only in one instance is there a strong possibility that both mother and baby were turned out, the mother going to live as a housekeeper for an elderly widowed gardener.

It was also a fact that the labourer's bride would often be several months pregnant. During 1840–61 seventy-two weddings took place amongst the labouring class at the Preston and Nutley churches. Twenty-three of these couples did not subsequently settle in the parish, but of the remaining forty-nine, just under half had their first child baptised within nine months of the wedding. This too had always been part of country life and a girl who married in haste was thought none the worst for it. She had at all events secured her man and the union was fertile.

No doubt there were cases where the match was not well chosen nor willingly undertaken by the groom. In one case at Nutley church the baptism of an illegitimate child took place just before the mother's wedding on the same day, the child being baptised in her maiden name. But the marriage usually held together in the parish at least. There were a few Preston-born wives in 1851 living in Winchester, Basingstoke and in a couple of nearby villages who had been deserted and forced to apply for Parish relief. This also happened to a Preston girl who left the village and married one George Burgess at Hammersmith in 1848, only to be left destitute five years later with their three children in Chiswick while George went off to become a private in the Staffordshire Militia.

In only a handful of households did the marriage prove to be childless. Usually new mouths were added at regular intervals and families of eight or more children were common. The record was held in these years by

63

Robert and Sarah Thorn, married in 1832, who lived in a cottage next to the yard at Lower Farm where they brought up fifteen children. Christian names would be chosen from a very narrow range—usually George, William, John, James, Henry, Eli or Joseph for the boys; and Sarah, Mary, Anne, Elizabeth, Martha, Ellen, Emma or Jane for the girls. Some children were given names which were clearly biblically inspired, like Adam, Moses, Noah, Solomon, Hephzibah, Manrah or Zacariah, but this fashion was not all that widespread. Twin boys were sometimes named Esau and Jacob, a twin boy and girl, Joseph and Mary. Two twin girls born to Thomas and Sarah Lynch were christened Love and Unity. Not that many of the names given to the boys were likely to be used much during their owner's lifetime—some nicknames given to people in the village, many of which probably date from this period, included Bucket, Pudden, Shacky, Bushy, Doughpuncher, Larkum, Skiver, Toady, Battle Axe, Eagle Beak, Giggy, Twarp and Boxer.

Most families in the 1850s could count themselves fortunate if they did not lose at least one child, particularly in early infancy. Of those 343 children baptised between 1840–61, twenty-five were to die within their first year, the numbers of boys and girls being almost equal. Once past the first year, the child's chances greatly improved, although a total of sixteen still died between their first and fifth birthday. Despite the crude conditions in most cottages, some advance was being made in the containment of the worst diseases. The fight against smallpox had been actively waged for several years. On January 28th 1823 the Vestry of Preston Candover, 'having taken into consideration the expediency of having the Children & Adults of the Parish Vaccinated in consequence of the Small Pox being prevalent at Wield & Bentworth, it was Resolved That Mr Thomas Woodward be sent to, & requested to come as early as he conveniently can, to Vaccinate all such as are disposed.' Woodward, a surgeon at Alton, came within a few days and vaccinated 229 people, most of them children. Such measures were also required in 1832 when Old George Lansley died from smallpox on May 27th. He was hurriedly buried at midnight on the same day and vaccinations were again carried out. Then there was typhus fever which broke out at Nutley in 1838 and carried off four people. The odd accident would also occur as in 1840 when Henry Oliver, aged five, was burnt to death and James Martin, aged ten, was killed by a horse and cart.

There were several families whose home had also been affected by the death of either or both parents. Those like Sarah Bulpitt who had no relatives living in the parish were in a less fortunate position than those who were part of an extended family. Mary, the mother of Elizabeth Wigg, when widowed in 1849 was able to bring her family to live in the home of her widowed father and her two unmarried brothers and thus look after them in return. Three orphan boys of the Goater family were taken in by their cousin, William Self. But there were limits to this kind of help and many had to struggle on as best they could. The hardships encouraged many widowed parents to remarry if possible. One man who did this three times during the course of his life was a shepherd named William Duffin, who lived in one half of the Cannon Down Cottages. When his second wife Maria died in 1858, he did the same as several other widowers and employed a housekeeper. At the Census of April 1861 this post was held by a girl of twenty-three named Sarah Aslett. William was fifty-one by then, but despite the thirty-year age gap, his housekeeper became his wife the following November.

*

A labourer's child growing up in the 1850s was likely to find home life uncomfortable and plain. The food would consist almost entirely of bread with potatoes, a scrap of bacon for Sunday, and very thin tea. The home would also be very crowded. Since the early 1800s the population of Preston and Nutley had increased by about 30 per cent, but the number of cottages had actually decreased. Three cottages housing six families had been demolished in the early 1840s in the park at Preston House and another two tenements were lost for the schoolroom. Even by 1823 several of the former yeomen's dwellings had been divided up into two or three tenements, like the farmhouses, Savages, Marshes and Nutley Court, and the same thing happened at Southwood Farm in the 1840s. The smaller cottages were divided up too, like one owned by John Whitear at Axford Corner and another on Tulls Hill, previously the home of a smallholder, Thomas Tull. When the latter died in 1827 the cottage was bought by one of the tradesmen and then subdivided into three tenements so crudely that only two of the families could use the original staircase, the third having to make do with a ladder up to the bedroom window.

(Left) Sarah, the wife of Jimmie Meachem. (Right) Dame Wigg in 1897. Born in 1829, her maiden name was Sarah Mills, a younger sister of Moses. She married Daniel Wigg in 1848 and lived next door to the Majors

Cottages changed hands frequently. In Preston parish only half of the sixty-two labouring families in 1851 had been living in the same cottage ten years before or were to be living in the same cottage ten years later. Few cottages had more than two bedrooms, and as the children grew up their home life would become increasingly cramped and irritating. If there were regular new additions to the family, then the parents would be even more keen to send the older ones out of the home once they were past school age. Thus, although families varied in size, the actual numbers of children living at home were fairly similar, the average size of each household being between four and five persons.

Frank and Susanna Hopkins who lived at Tulls Hill Cottages had eight sons who all left home in their turn. The eldest son William was the first, becoming a servant down at Manor Farm; by 1851 he had left the parish.

His younger brothers were working by then; John and Ben still at home, George and Young Frank lodging at Southwood Farm. They too left the parish during the 1850s and by 1861 only the youngest son Bobby was left, a servant at the Croft. There were many others like the Hopkins boys who left the parish at some stage. A few probably tried their luck by tramping round the farms of the district, but quite a number would have gone to the hiring fair at Basingstoke, held on October 11th of each year. Thus a number of men born in Preston and Nutley were to be found in 1851 living as farm servants in those parishes within the ambit of the Basingstoke Fair—Monk Sherbourne, Ellisfield, Wield, Bradley, Farleigh and Dummer. Conversely, many of the farm servants living on the farms of Preston and Nutley in 1851 had been born in these particular parishes and they too would have been hired in the same way.

For the daughter of a labouring family it was virtually impossible to earn a reasonable wage and still live at home. Within a year or two of leaving school her mother would seek a place for her as a servant to one of the local farmers, shopkeepers or tradesmen. The really ambitious mother, however, would want her daughter to progress to gentlemen's service, for which she would be reliant on the vicar, the shopkeepers or farmers who would, for instance, be able to tell her of notices they had read in the *Hampshire Chronicle*, such as the one that appeared in December 1859:

> WANTED, in a Clergyman's Family in SOUTHAMPTON—A very respectable, strong, active, young Woman as UNDER LAUNDRY MAID, and to assist in the House Work. She must understand Laundry work sufficiently to give a good help, and be willing to learn House work if she has not yet been in service.

Such vacancies would occur only rarely in the big houses of the parish. The numbers employed in 1851 at Preston House, North and South Hall, and Preston Cottage amounted to twenty-three people, of whom nine came from other parts of Hampshire and the rest from towns and villages throughout Southern England. The girls from Preston families, therefore, were sent off at the age of thirteen upwards and in 1851 they could be found in such residences as Dummer House, Beech Hill House at Stratfield Saye, the Rectory at Lasham, and Hoddington House at Upton

Grey. Most were in the lower grades of the servant hierarchy and as they progressed they would often go to places outside the county, especially to London.

Some of the boys or girls who left the parish would remain single and in service all their lives, but most would get married at some stage. Some would already be engaged to partners back home. Joe Alexander, a servant at a farm in Monk Sherbourne in March 1851, returned to Preston in May 1852 for his marriage to a local girl, Elizabeth Whatmore. Similarly Maria Edwards, in service at Winchester to the Chief Constable of Hampshire in 1851, had returned to Preston by October 1855 and was married to the son of a Nutley family. For such couples the courtship was often long and their chances to meet were few. Those who were still un-fettered would perhaps be better off, like James Stevens from Wield who worked for John Whitear and who courted Mary Parker, a servant at John Thorp's. Another servant girl of John Thorp's, Lucy Aslett, married his apprentice butcher, William Smith, in November 1861.

Thus many couples met while in service, and this meant that of all the marriages in the labouring classes at the Preston and Nutley churches between 1840–61, only 32 per cent were between the children of two local families. The outsider was usually the groom and thus those weddings where just the bride was from a local family amounted to 44 per cent. Several of these girls of course may have only returned to Preston for the wedding itself, like Ellen Bramley who in March 1851 was employed as a cook at Hoddington House and who was married at Preston in the September to a gardener from Greywell. The 4 per cent of weddings where neither bride nor groom had any family in the parish, were usually between servants who had become engaged while at Preston. This happened to Ben Ansell, a labourer from East Meon who in April 1861 was in lodgings at the bottom of Tulls Hill, and Ellen Cook from Middle Wallop, who was a servant for the Reverend Wickham at South Hall. They were married in the November.

*

Many Preston-born men who married a girl in another part of Hampshire came back home to live soon afterwards. This had been so for many years and thus in 1851 out of a total of one hundred households, only twenty-three included both husband and wife who had been born in Preston or Nutley. In nearly half the households only the husband had been born in either of the two parishes. The birthplaces of those wives born elsewhere lay mostly within a five to ten mile radius of Preston and thus, although in most families the relatives living in the two parishes would be on the husband's side, the wife's relatives would not live a great distance away.

A life of hard toil would face the young couple as they in turn struggled to bring up a family, and it would bring them few rewards as they approached old age. James Duffin, for instance, fifty-five years old in 1851, had started work at the age of eight helping a shepherd on Nutley Down. He led a third team of horses when he was ten and was second carter at fourteen on a farm at Dummer. After he married his wife Charlotte, he came back to Nutley and worked as head carter at Manor Farm for about twenty-five years. Then he had a serious illness and thereafter was never able to get regular work. On becoming a widower in the 1840s, he moved in with his married daughter at the Old Marshes Farmhouse and earnt a few pence by doing odd jobs, like breaking up stones for roadmending. Others did the same, like Sylvanus Thorn who kept the churchyard tidy. Some old soldiers had an army pension to eke out their family budgets; James Clark and Charles Pink at Nutley were both Chelsea Pensioners. Life was possibly most difficult for the seven elderly couples who lived alone and had no family, and for whom the workhouse must have been a constant threat.

As long as they remained in the village, each labouring family could expect little improvement. Several must have gone to search for better opportunities in the towns, for during the 1850s the labouring population fell by 20 per cent. Emigration was excluded for many people unless they could be assisted with the cost of the passage. This happened to the family of William Parker. Born in 1800, he worked as a young boy on a farm and then became an apprentice at the brickyard. In 1829 he married a local girl, Maria Blake, and in the succeeding years they raised ten children. They were at this time staunch members of the Church of England; Maria ran the school at the rectory and William was the parish clerk, sexton, bell-ringer and gravedigger. Then in 1851 a Mormon missionary from America, William Budge, appeared in the village looking for

69

converts and Maria Parker was soon won over to the new faith. Others followed her example and were baptised it seems in a pond in Wield Wood—the Cannons and Duffins at Cannon Down Cottages, the Selfs, Huttons, and some of the Alexanders. The effect on the village must have been quite dramatic but most of the outrage seems to have fallen on the Parkers, mainly because of their former close connections with the

William and Maria Parker

Established Church. The clergy made several attempts to dissuade Maria from the new faith but she refused and in fact went on to have all the children baptised too. Her unwavering attitude led to her dismissal as a teacher. William not only lost his job as parish clerk but was sacked from the brickyard by the Fitzgeralds and evicted from his cottage.

The Mormons ran an immigration fund and Maria persuaded the two eldest sons George, who had a wife and two children, and Charles to emigrate to Utah. Another family living at Upper Barn, George and Eliza Alexander and their two children, also agreed to go and the party set sail on the *Golconda* in February 1854. On arriving at New Orleans, they were sent with other Mormons by boat to St Louis from where they eventually set out for Utah taking a herd of wild Texan cattle with them. The

(Left) Bobby Hopkins—born 1842, he was living with his parents in 1851 at Tulls Hill Cottages. In later life he became very crippled with rheumatism and died at the Basingstoke Infirmary. (Right) Moses Mills; born 1826, he married Mary Collins from Binstead in 1849 and in 1851 they and their small son Simon were living as lodgers with Moses' brother Daniel and his family near Oxells Farm. In later life he lived with Bobby Hopkins, both men being widowers. When too old to manage on his own, he went to live at Micheldever where he died

cattle were difficult to manage for these former Hampshire farmhands and Indians caused frequent stampedes. The party also suffered from cholera and mountain fever; Eliza Alexander was buried on the Plains and her

North Hall Cottages, the home of the Parker family

husband died soon after reaching Utah, their children being adopted by the Parkers. Soon after their arrival in October 1854, Brigham Young, the Mormon President, sent them out into the country near the Great Salt Lake to begin a new settlement. The hardships continued; in the first winter their cattle froze to death and in the next six years most of their crops were destroyed by grasshoppers.

Back home in England, the rest of the Parker family had left Preston but continued to be hounded for their Mormon faith wherever they tried to settle. Several of the other children emigrated at intervals to Utah and finally in June 1863 William, Maria and the three youngest children sailed from London in the packet ship *Amazon*. From New York they set out for Utah, travelling across the Plains with an ox-team. Though very ill on the journey, William survived and settled at Salt Lake City where he worked at making adobe and weaving willow fences. Maria died in 1869, William in 1883. Despite all their hardships, the others eventually prospered and can have had few regrets at exchanging the green downs of Hampshire for the arid deserts of Utah.

George Parker (1830–1920), *eldest son of William and Maria Parker, in about* 1897, *by which time he had given up farming and was a coal-dealer at Ogden, near Salt Lake City. With him is his second wife. His first wife, Mary Lewis, made him promise that after her death he would return to England and marry her widowed sister, which he did*

Quite a few members of the mid-Victorian labouring class, however, remained in the Preston area all their lives, the last survivor being Mrs Fanny Thorne. She was born in 1862, the fourth child of Henry and Emily Lynch, and grew up in a cottage close by the green. She did hardly any schooling but worked from an early age in the fields, helping her father bind corn and stook the sheaves. Her husband, Colour-Sergeant Thorne, died when she was still quite young and left her with a large family. She worked on the land to support them and continued to do so to a remarkable age, first at Moundsmere, walking there and back from Axford till she was nearly seventy. Then, when the doctor told her the work and distance were too much for her, she came to live at Preston and worked on a poultry farm. Then she went to help out at Home Farm (formerly Preston Farm), stooking a field of corn by herself at the age of eighty-eight. Her efforts did not pass unnoticed, however, for in 1951 she was awarded the British Empire Medal for fifty years work on the land. It was a festive occasion; the church bells were rung, a guard of honour was formed by the British Legion and the village hall was packed to capacity. Thirty-seven of Fanny's relatives were amongst the gathering. Fanny herself, flanked by the Parish Council, was on stage to receive the medal from the Lord Lieutenant of the County, the Duke of Wellington, and to hear him read out the following message from the King:

> I greatly regret that I am unable to give you personally the award which you have so well earned. I now send it to you with my congratulations and my best wishes for your future happiness.— (Signed) George R. to Mrs Fanny Thorne, B.E.M.

In all, it was an honour that Henry and Emily Lynch were unlikely to have foreseen for their daughter. Fanny died in March 1961, just a year short of her hundredth birthday.

Mrs Fanny Thorne with her British Empire Medal in March 1951. *With her are the Parish Council; (from left) Mr R. Whitworth, Mr G. Westbrook, Miss E. Aris, Mrs D. D. Cosier, Mr W. Murphy, and Mr G. Elbourne*

9

The Poor Law

When people in the labouring class in Preston Candover were faced with sickness or destitution, they had to turn for help to a body known as 'The Parish'. This had often been the case—for instance, with Robert Bye. Born in 1786, his early life had been spent as a yearly servant on several farms in Preston before he left to find work in Basingstoke. He was married there in 1810 and a few years later, when he fell ill, his wife Olive came to Preston to obtain relief from the Parish. The money was sent regularly for about twelve weeks, including the payment of a doctor's bill for 40/-. During the next ten years or more, although the couple continued to live in Basingstoke, they frequently received relief and medical attendance paid for by Preston Parish, as in 1826 when Robert was ill for several weeks with smallpox. Then in 1834 the Parish Officers had them brought to Preston where they remained for a couple of years and then they were provided with a cottage at Nutley. Until his death in 1847, Robert was frequently granted relief, mainly for asthma.

The system which supported Robert Bye was known as the Poor Law. It had its origins in the reign of Elizabeth I when the duty of relieving poverty had been left to each parochial authority. The money came from rates which fell on real property and from Tithes, and its distribution was handled by one of the Parish Officers called the Overseer. The Poor Law survived till the 1830s as a parish responsibility and some idea of how it worked in Preston can be gained from the Vestry Minute Book:

May 26th 1823: Resolved that Ann Allen be allowed the usual Parish allowance of a Gallon of Bread and sixpence.

December 18th 1823: Resolved that a Round Frock be given to Ann Hutton's son but that he must not expect any more, at any future time.

April 19th 1824: It was agreed that Dinah Baldwin's Boy be allowed a Hat, a pr Trousers & shirt. That 10/- be given to Charles Blake, he having been unable to Work for the last five weeks from Illness.

Clearly the Poor Law had become a highly informal system, and in the years after 1815 the necessity for reform became acute. This was finally achieved in the Poor Law Amendment Act of 1834, under which the type of assistance given previously in Preston was called outdoor relief and would in future be granted only to those unable to work because of old age or a spell of sickness. The destitute able-bodied labourer would receive help in the form of indoor relief, by which his family would be placed in a special workhouse, as would orphaned children and the old and sick who could not be relieved at home. Parishes were to be grouped into Unions and the paid officials would be supervised by elected Boards of Guardians. It is well known of course how the amended Poor Law, in the early years at least, was enforced with considerable severity.

The parishes of Preston Candover and Nutley came to be included within the Poor Law Union of Basingstoke. Each parish levied a Poor Rate on property at one shilling in the pound, collected by the Overseers four times a year in Preston and once a year in Nutley. Preston's representative on the Board of Guardians was William Lainson, Nutley's was William Blatch. The workhouse was situated in open country about half a mile to the east of Basingstoke. It consisted of several blocks arranged around four courtyards and included an infirmary, school, chapel, dormitories and workplaces. The layout was arranged so that not only were the sexes kept apart but also the adults were separated from the children, and thus families were immediately split up. The work given to the paupers usually consisted of stone-breaking, hand-grinding of corn, oakum-picking and bone-grinding. Behind the workhouse were vegetable gardens while at the front stood a tall block where the staff lived: a porter, nurse, schoolmaster and schoolmistress, a matron, and the Master of the

Workhouse, who in 1851 was a thirty-six-year-old gentleman named John Harbour.

Despite the daunting presence of the workhouse, it is difficult to tell how many people in a single parish would ever have to live inside its gates. In 1851, when the number of inmates in the Basingstoke Workhouse was nearly 300, only eight had been born in Preston and Nutley. Between March and September 1848 there were forty-three people who received poor relief but only five of them were actually kept in the workhouse. Two were elderly paupers: Tom Baldwin aged sixty-six and Joseph Tibble aged seventy-four, and both men were eventually to die there. The Baldwin family had disappeared from the village by the 1850s but the Tibbles were still there, so presumably Joseph was too sickly to be cared for by his family. Of the other three cases in 1848, one was an orphan girl of five named Ann Thorp, the others Thomas and Harriet Greenaway, a brother and sister in their twenties whose family lived at Lower Farm. Thomas had left the workhouse by 1851 but Harriet was still there, though the reason for this is not clear. On the whole, however, indoor relief does seem to have been used only in exceptional circumstances.

*

Though many powers of the individual parish had been terminated in 1834, the Overseer still had a strong influence, for most labourers needed outdoor relief at some stage. Until September 1847 the Poor Law Minute Books of the Basingstoke Union recorded all the instances of outdoor relief granted in each parish, and in the eighty-two months between December 1840 and September 1847, a total of sixty-seven individuals in Preston and Nutley were granted relief at some time. Fifty-three of them were married men. Thus about half of the hundred labouring households needed help during this period. The strict rules of the Poor Law meant that they would only receive help in times of dire necessity when all their own funds had been exhausted; thus 84 per cent of the men granted relief received it in no more than four of these eighty-two months.

Of the total 140 cases where relief was granted in those eighty-two months, over 80 per cent were caused by the breadwinner's illness. The records usually termed every complaint as being due to 'debility', but occasionally the Overseer was more explicit: abcess in foot, heart affection,

77

erysipelas, quinsey, lumbago, vertigo, fits. The amount of relief granted would increase markedly during the winter months due to colds, influenza and rheumatism. Sometimes there would be accidents, as in 1844 when William Oliver received relief for a fracture and William Alexander was paid 14/- to cover the expenses of a nurse for an amputation.

The Overseer would give relief in both money and food, according to the number of children under sixteen in the breadwinner's family. For instance, in 1841 Thomas Nicholson with a wife and four children received 3/- and four gallons of bread each week while he was suffering from an 'affection of the bowels', while Jack Thorn had 3/- and 3/7*d* in food for his family of five while recovering from an 'injury in the side'. George Whatmore, a bachelor, received two pounds of mutton weekly for an 'affection of the heart'. If necessary the Overseer would send for one of the Union's Medical Officers. These men, known generally as the Pauper's Doctors, had a poor reputation and this seems to have been the case with the officer responsible for Preston and Nutley, Mr Perry. In 1844 William Blatch complained to the Board of Guardians that Perry had not sent a bottle of medicine to one pauper as had been arranged and on another occasion he neglected to pay a second visit to a patient whose bandages he had applied too tightly. Mr Perry, however, could usually give the Guardians an explanation.

Relief was granted for other things besides sickness and old age. A small sum was paid out each month to Esther Adams, fifthy-seven years old in 1851 and a lodger in a cramped cottage near Tulls Hill. She was labelled a 'lunatic pauper', though apparently not dangerous enough to be sent to an asylum. During 1840–47 there were some seventeen cases where relief was granted to a husband so that he could stay home and look after his family while his wife was in confinement. And then there was James Oliver who received 11/6*d* for 'funeral expenses' in April 1846 after having buried both his wife and son within the space of a month.

As with Robert and Olive Bye, the Overseer could help a poor family by finding them accommodation and for a number of years the Parish had owned certain cottages for this purpose. One of them was situated at the bottom of Tulls Hill while two others lay alongside the road near Axford. These latter cottages were rebuilt by the Parish in 1840 at a total cost of £48. They were reserved for the very poorest and at one time the

78

Overseers were not too bothered about collecting the rents. Nonetheless, there was little comfort in a Parish Cottage for the pauper families were packed in. The cottages at Axford in 1851 held nine families, a total of fifty-one people, while two families were crammed into the tiny cottage at Tulls Hill.

The provision of poor relief fell on about 15 per cent of all householders in the two parishes, who generally felt that their burden was unduly heavy. In parishes such as Brown and Chilton Candover where virtually all the land was owned by the Barings, it was possible to pull down any empty cottages so that potential paupers would be forced to move on. This was far more difficult in Preston where many cottages were bought up by tradesmen who derived a steady income from their rents. It would seem, however, that during the late 1850s steps were taken to lessen the rate burden and one way of doing this was to reduce the amount of accommodation provided by the parish. A minute of a vestry meeting held in 1858 reads: 'It was agreed that the two cottages belonging to the Parish now inhabited by Nicholson and T. Wigg should be made into one'. (This was one of the Axford cottages.) The Parish Officers really wanted to dispose of the cottages altogether; a minute of 1859 reads: 'It was agreed that Mr Lunn should be requested to lay the case of the Parish Cottages before the proper authorities and that, if permission should be granted, they should be pulled down'. This did not in fact happen at that time although the number of occupants was reduced; in 1861 there were only fifteen people in the Axford cottages.

Most of the poor families put into the Parish Cottages remained there for several years, like those of Henry Hutton, Tom Wigg, George Martin, James Knight, William Oliver and Tom Nicholson. The latter two men had actually helped build the Axford cottages in 1840. Tom Wigg suffered from very poor health; he was granted relief in seventeen of those eighty-two months during 1840–47, far more than most other men in the parish. In his mid-thirties by 1848, he had seen his family grow to eight children and, in order to reduce his relief money, he was required in 1847 to place one of his daughters in the workhouse. His neighbour, James Knight, applied for relief in thirteen of the eighty-two months and also had one of his daughters actually born in the workhouse in 1846.

These men could usually find only seasonal work on the land and in

79

winter their main source of employment was the repair of the public roads, which at that time was the responsibility of the Parish. The levying of a Highway Rate at threepence in the pound and the organisation of the work was the responsibility of the Surveyor of the Highways. Two farmers held this post in Preston, one in Nutley. Some gravel and chalk pits had been reserved in 1823 for the surveyor's use, though the chief material used was flint collected from off the fields. Work would begin in about November and carry on until April. The flints would be gathered by groups of women and children, whose rate of pay would be threepence a ton, and dumped in heaps by the roadside. A man would then be paid sixpence a ton to break up the flints, and the chippings were then taken in a hand-cart to the spot where the road needed repairing. For repair work a man could earn one shilling a day.

Stone-picking above Nutley Manor Farm

The amount of work done would vary from year to year. The accounts which survive for Preston parish show that in the season 1849–50 the total expenses came to over £37, whereas in the following season £17 was spent and only £7 in the season following that. The numbers employed would vary: a total of fifteen men were hired for day labour in 1849–50, five in 1850–51, and nine in 1851–52, some throughout the season and others for odd days. Seven people were hired to collect materials in 1849–50, none were required in 1851–52. The system was, therefore, highly informal, the surveyor finding a job where possible for any labourer who was out of work. The 1849–50 season could have entailed a back-log of repairs, but it is also probable that a lot of men were unemployed that

80

winter. The names of the fathers who lived in the Parish Cottages appear frequently in the Highway Accounts, and sometimes other members of the family too; in March 1851 Henry Hutton earnt 4/- repairing Tulls Hill Lane with flints broken up by Tom Nicholson which the latter's wife and children had collected from the fields along the Chilton Road in December. In Nutley there was a team of women who were regularly employed stone-picking and sometimes at stone-breaking as well. In February 1852 Letty Duffin, then fifty-nine years old, spent five days breaking stones while Rachel Goodyear did the same for seventeen days in March 1857 when she was nearly seventy; in all, a hard price to pay to stay out of the workhouse.

Stone-breaking and road-mending along Berrydown Lane, close to the cottage at Blackburn's Farm, Axford

The Parish would only grant relief to someone who was their responsibility, and how that should be defined had been set down in a sixteenth century Act called the Law of Settlement which made every pauper chargeable upon and removable to his 'place of settlement'. This was very often the parish of his birth, but he could gain a settlement and become chargeable to a new parish if he succeeded in staying there for a whole year. This was the main reason why young men returned home after marrying in another parish and also why empty cottages were sometimes demolished.

A set procedure had been evolved to deal with paupers like William Aslett who in the winter of 1855 became destitute at Alton with his wife and six children. The whole family was put into the Alton Workhouse and on being questioned, William told the Overseers that in 1817, 'being un-married and without child or children, I was hired as a yearly servant by Richard Hammond of Moundsmere Farm, and during the whole year slept and lodged in the parish of Preston Candover'. He did this in the two succeeding years as well and therefore the Overseers deduced that Preston was William Aslett's place of settlement. They then filled in a printed form called an Order of Removal and posted it to the Overseers of Preston, requesting them to take charge of the pauper and his family.

It was a problem that faced Preston's Overseers on several occasions during the '40s and '50s. A couple of months after Robert Bye died at Nutley in February 1847, Olive went back to live in Basingstoke and in early June she applied for relief to the Relieving Officer of the Basingstoke District. Since she was Preston's responsibility, he sent off an Order of Removal. Preston Parish duly paid her relief money, though they did not consider it necessary to have her actually brought back to the village. This often happened, especially in cases of sickness; of the thirty-eight people granted outdoor relief between March and September 1848, eight were living in other parishes, mostly in Basingstoke.

The Overseers of Preston also received an Order of Removal in the case of Charles Blake who in 1842 became destitute with his wife and three children in Titchfield and was subsequently put in the Fareham Workhouse. Charles had been born in Preston in 1811, married a girl from Wield in 1833, and four years later went off to work as a railway navvy. His daughter Ann was born in 1839 at Basingstoke, his son James at Titchfield some five months before they were put in the Fareham Workhouse. Charles was twice granted relief by Preston after he left the parish and did nothing to gain a new settlement in his own right. The Fareham Overseers, therefore, soon despatched the Blakes home to Preston.

Preston Parish in its turn was troubled by paupers from elsewhere. One such man was an elderly labourer named Thomas Chandler who was taken ill while staying in the village in 1843 and had to be maintained at Preston's expense in the Basingstoke Workhouse. The Overseers learnt that he was about eighty years of age and had been born at Woodborough in Wiltshire. His place of settlement was Manningford Bruce where he had been hired as an odd boy by the local vicar in 1780 and where he had spent most of his life. Preston's Overseers promptly sent off an Order of Removal.

Ascertaining a person's place of settlement could be a complex business and disputes easily arose, as happened in the case of James Martin. Born in Preston in 1809, he appears to have left home in his late teens, joined the Army and went to serve in India. He returned to England in about 1840 and eventually found his way back to Preston where in 1844 the Overseers issued an Order to have him and his family removed to North Waltham which they considered to be his place of settlement. The North Waltham Overseers did not agree and threatened to prosecute an appeal against the Order at the General Quarter Sessions at Winchester. A meeting was quickly arranged at which North Waltham eventually recognised its responsibility in the matter and the appeal was thus dropped. Preston Parish, however, found itself prosecuting an appeal in 1855 over the case of Jeremiah Self, the former village butcher who was now an elderly pauper living in Odiham and for whom Preston considered itself no longer responsible.

Sometimes the village would be visited by other people who belonged to the rootless class of gipsies, vagrants and beggars. Such people rarely figure in any documents of the period, but on Census night in 1851 the Enumerator for Herriard discovered a number of gipsies living in huts on Herriard Common. Several of them he described simply as beggar, vagabond or tramp, but others had a profession: John Palmer was a besom-maker, Richard Green a chairmender, and four of his sons strolling sweeps. There were eight children in the Green family and their wandering life is well seen in the list of birthplaces: Sherfield, Odiham, Herriard, Odiham, Hartley Row, Sherbourne, Odiham and Micheldever. Several of these parishes had commons where the gipsies could camp and perhaps they sometimes stopped on Oakhills Common in Preston too. Certainly such gipsies must have been a familiar sight in the village, knocking at the doors and offering to sweep chimneys, mend chairs or perhaps to sell a few besoms.

10

The Charities

> I am, and have been for many years, sensible of the very great distress prevalent generally among the lower class of people and am now, as I have been, most willingly inclined to contribute to their relief.

Thus George Purefoy Jervoise commenced a letter to the Curate of Preston Candover in November 1830. By this time the village charities had become numerous and complicated. There was one which derived from a man whose actual identity had long been forgotten but who had once given some land to the poor of the parish which produced 10/- a year. John Thorp's family had inherited this land and continued to distribute the money each year between three deserving old men of the parish. Similarly a sum of £5 had been given by another forgotton figure and vested in Thomas Hall, producing 5/- a year. Lipscomb's Gift, a rent charge of £4 a year, derived from the will of Robert Lipscomb, dated 1711. These latter charities were paid for by the Jervoises and distributed in sums of a few shillings each amongst the deserving poor of the parish—which usually meant those people who had managed to keep on the right side of the vicar and churchwardens.

Few charities, however, involved giving actual money to the poor but more often fuel and clothes, such as the annual gift of red flannel for petticoats to the six oldest widows at Christmas time. Oakhills Common too was organised as a charity where the cottagers were allowed to cut so many cords of firewood in the presence of a charity trustee. It was said that the Common had been bequeathed to the poor of Preston Candover by two maiden ladies in a remote period, but Sumner Wilson's researches into this and the other charities were unable to find any basis for such a tradition.

Apart from these traditional charities, there were others organised on an annual basis, and the curate, Robert Wedgwood, had the accounts of 1840 specially printed so as 'to remind us of our great duty to remember the Poor and make us forward therein' as well as prove 'to the Poor of Preston Candover and Nutley that they have not been forgotten'. Firstly there were Clubs for fuel and for adult and children's clothing which, though assisted by the gentry, clergy and a few of the farmers, were based on a regular payment by the members. In the Adult Clothing Club these payments came to 3/8d a year and in the Fuel Club 4/6d. This tended to put such Clubs out of reach of the very poor and so for them the answer was a subscription. There were two of these in 1840; one being 'A Subscription on behalf of the Sufferers from Fire', the other for 'Supplying the Poor with Fuel and Clothing at Reduced Price'.

The organisation of the charities was one of the Reverend Wickham's duties. In 1853 he collected £57.14.3½d for a Clothing Fund, of which some £19 had been contributed by Miss Blunt, Mrs Fitzgerald and Charles Rumbold. Wickham himself put in two guineas, his curate one guinea. A Coal Fund produced £29.1.0d of which £12 came from the upper class. In distributing the Clothing Fund, Wickham saw that each subscriber received goods at a rate of 10/- in the pound beyond what he paid, apart from certain elderly people who were supplied with articles of clothing gratuitously. In the Coal Fund the fuel was purchased mainly from Wolf Brothers of Andover and carted out from Basingstoke station by the farmers who delivered four hundredweight of coal gratuitously to every poor family in Preston and Nutley.

It was difficult of course to decide who amongst the poor was most in need of such goods. As Wickham wrote to one of his contributors in February 1856:

'I have at last been able to distribute the money, which you were kind enough to desire should be given to the poor. 36 families had flannel or sheeting to the amount of 3/6d each & 50 flannel, a sheet, or stockings

85

to the amount of 1/6*d* each' I have spread the money over a larger space than you may have expected, as you desired that it should be given to the *poorest*. But I found it a great difficulty to lessen the number, without giving offence as the people really are very poor, and no-one is willing to allow that any body is poorer than himself.'

Thus of the hundred or so labouring families in Preston and Nutley, eighty-six were considered to be in need of charity. How easy it was to obtain contributions is not clear, though Wickham did once write: 'It is not uncommon to find that, when aid is applied for towards those charities, it is granted, if at all, as a personal favour to me.'

The vicar, therefore, was in a somewhat unenviable position over the charities. Sumner Wilson took over their organisation when he came to Preston, but during the 1880s many of them died out, the money being swallowed up in building the new church. At any rate, that is what was alleged in a number of rumours.

*

For certain men in the village a more dignified form of assistance than the Parish existed when they fell ill, and that was the Preston Candover Benevolent Society. It had been instituted in 1832 and was to be overhauled in later years by the Oddfellows Friendly Society. Its objects were relief in sickness, payment for medical attendance, and payment of a sum of money on the death of a member or his wife. It was run by various elected members: stewards, treasurer, trustees, a management committee and a secretary, who for many years was Daniel Light. Meetings were held in the schoolroom once a month. To join the Society a man had to be aged between sixteen and thirty-five and sign a declaration that he was not afflicted with any disease or infirmity. He paid an admission fee of 2/6*d*, subscription of 1/9*d* a month, and at the end of six months he became entitled to all the benefits of the Society. These were that if he fell ill, he would receive 8/- a week for four months and 4/- a week for any longer time. When a member died the Society would pay his widow £5 and the stewards would attend his funeral to see that he was decently buried.

There were some very strict rules about giving benefit from the funds. A member could only receive an allowance if he was one 'whom it shall please God to afflict with sickness or accident', and this did not include an

86

injury sustained by 'mobbing, wrestling, fighting, backsword or any un-lawful conduct, or anyone who has any venereal disease'. A member would be expelled if he returned to work after the initial four-month period before he was perfectly recovered, just to be placed on the sick list after a short interval. He would also be excluded if he was discovered to be 'engaged in any immoral or unlawful pursuit, be found in a state of in-toxication, or pretending illness'. Furthermore, 'if any sick member be known to visit public houses, gin, or beer-shops, while he is receiving benefit from the fund' he would forfeit 5/-. The Society also used fines to ensure good standards of behaviour at meetings: 'If any member curse, swear, take God's name in vain, offer to lay a wager, play at any game, or refuse to keep silence when ordered by the stewards' he would forfeit 6d; for quarrelling or striking another—fined 2/6d; reflecting 'upon another for lawfully receiving benefit from funds'—fined 5/-. Inevitably the Socie-ty became the preserve of the shopkeepers, craftsmen and the better-off labourers. As has been seen, during much of the 1840s over half the labouring families had to apply to the Parish when the breadwinner was ill, so clearly the Society was of no benefit to them.

On the first Monday in July the Society held an annual meeting which was known as Club Day. The secretary and stewards would meet at eight o'clock in the morning to settle the business of the Society, and then the members would arrive at nine to receive their dividend. From there every member was expected to attend divine service. After that the main event of the day would begin, as stated in the rule book:

A good dinner, &c., will be provided, for which every member who partakes thereof shall pay a reasonable demand to be decided on the meeting night previous to the annual feast. That a sufficient quantity of beer be provided for each member and at no time to exceed three quarts per member. That the clergyman of the parish of Preston Can-dover shall be requested to preach a sermon on the occasion. A band of music shall be hired for the occasion, and a bower erected, and the money collected at the same to go towards defraying the expenses of the band. All the members shall march two and two, in order as their names stand on the register, immediately after the band, when called upon by the steward so to do.

For most people life offered few diversions from work and such events as Club Day were seized on readily. For sporting excitment one could watch the local hunt, go to the racecourse on Abbotstone Down, or else walk out to Preston Down to watch the cricket club in action; one of the oldest clubs in Hampshire and very proud of its tradition. Usually, however, it was a subscription which enabled some event to be celebrated. This was done, for instance, when Nutley Church was opened in 1845, so that bread and cheese could be given away to the poor at the gate. To celebrate Queen Victoria's wedding to Prince Albert on February 10th 1840, Robert Wedgwood raised a subscription of £27.16.0*d* with which he bought 572 lbs of meat and suet from John Thorp, 56 gallons of flour and 112 lbs of raisins from George Allen and James Marshall, and 57 gallons of beer (costing 2*d* a pint) from Mr Hunt at the New Inn. All this he then shared out between 458 people.

Then too there would be such celebrations as the Harvest Dinner, held in the schoolroom under the auspices of gentry and clergy. A report survives of one such occasion and, though it actually took place in 1867, the sentiments surrounding it would no doubt have been the same a few years earlier. At the dinner itself, for instance, the health of Mr Fitzgerald was proposed and received with enthusiasm, upon which he:

> expressed the pleasure which it gave him as a resident Landlord to have been instrumental in their bringing together the whole parish rich and poor to thank God for and rejoice over the safe gathering in of the harvest. The health of the farmers by whose unaided liberality the labourers were entertained was then heartily proposed and a few effective words spoken by several of the employees. . . . After dinner many adjourned to the school room where an admirable collection of flowers and vegetables was to be seen. The prizes were distributed by Madame de Gilbert of Preston House assisted by Mr Fitzgerald and great interest was felt in the two prizes for tidy gardens falling to two widows, Mrs W. Hutton of Preston and Goodyear of Nutley. Though the fruit was very scanty owing to the late frost, some first rate vegetables were exhibited and a most interesting display of flowers, contributed by children, labourers, shopkeepers and in fact all classes, filled the schoolroom which was, with the church, very tastefully decorated.

After a pleasant evening enlivened by the band and a satisfactory allowance of good beer, the National Anthem was played about nine o'clock and between ten and eleven all had returned happily and soberly home.

And thus fortified, the villagers would emerge next morning ready to face the dull daily round once more.

11

A Hundred Years On

It was in 1870 that Preston Candover first acquired its cast iron parish pump, erected on the village green under the auspices of Colonel Fitzgerald and dug by one of the Olivers for £3. In a dry summer there would be a continuous procession of water-carts coming down from Wield and Ellisfield to fill up from the pump. Religious and political meetings would be held around it while pedlars would display their wares on the brick steps. The Fitzgeralds also financed the building of the Purefoy Arms which replaced the New Inn in the 1860s. The church was consecrated in 1885, and a memorial erected in 1919 to the sixteen men of the parish who fell in the Great War. And then in the 1920s the Parish Council decided to have the smelly old pond filled in and turfed over, thus at long last giving Preston a proper village green.

Over the past hundred years such piecemeal changes have gradually altered the appearance of the village. Its society has changed radically too. Within only a few years after the 1850s, the farming prosperity was brought to an end by cheap American wheat flooding the home market and this, together with growing opportunities in the towns, led to an exodus of young people from the land which has continued ever since. Today the total population in the two parishes is about half that of 1851 and the majority of people are middle-aged or elderly. The number of houses though has roughly doubled and they mostly contain only two people where very often two families once crammed themselves in.

The estates of Preston and Nutley remained large in size, though sales often brought about different groupings of farms. The Preston House Estate was bought by Lord Templemore in 1877 and then ten years later by the Hope family who sold certain parts of it in 1909, including Home Farm and Preston House. The Jervoise connection with the area ended in 1905 when the estates were sold by Admiral Purefoy. The Moundsmere Estate was acquired on a long lease from Winchester College in 1908 by Mr Wilfred Buckley, a prominent dairy farmer who built the large Palladian style Moundsmere Manor and developed a model dairy farm of wide renown. The tenant farmers elsewhere in the valley, however, made do with old buildings and implements. The binder had appeared in the 1880s, a few Fordson tractors in the 1920s, but there were few other such changes until the Second World War. Today agriculture in the valley is highly mechanised and employs only about a quarter of the working people; far more, especially the young, travel to work each day to shops, factories and offices in Basingstoke, Alresford and even further afield.

The Venture Bus Company which began a regular service in 1926, was one of many influences which broke down the isolation of the village. The old Turnpike (renamed the B.3046) and several other roads were finally macadamised in the late 1930s. Electricity reached Preston in 1939, piped water in 1947. A public telephone was installed as early as 1910 in the greenhouse alongside the post office at the Vines' former shop. The village had a resident doctor who lived in the Old Rectory until 1914 and after that a doctor from Alresford used to travel out twice a week—at first on a motor-cycle and later in a car—and hold his surgery at the Forge Cottage in the room which had once been Rachel Whitear's beershop. Then there was the carrier, Jack Chivers, who shortly after the Great War replaced his two mules with a secondhand Ford van and later with a lorry.

The breakdown of isolation had its effect on the village shops. The Thorps continued to be the butchers until John Thorp, the great-grandson of John Thorp senior, died during the influenza epidemic of 1918. The Allens' shop closed down soon after the family emigrated to Canada in the early 1900s. The Vines' former shop, however, has survived and so has a shop established by the dealer, Charles Mercer, in the 1860s and known today as 'Cantertons'. In the 1920s the latter shop baked their own bread, but this came to an end once the Co-op and other large bakers from the towns started making deliveries. It also sold items like footwear and drapery at one time, but this in turn was usurped by the big stores whose travellers would tour round the villages with a wagonette full of samples from which the people could make their choice. They too disappeared once people could travel into town on the buses.

Along with better transport came cheap factory-made goods, both of which gradually put the local craftsmen out of business. By 1900 the tailor had gone, though the shoemaker continued a little longer—Bill Prior, a short club-footed man who had been taught his trade by Jeremiah Chamberlain. The last carpenter and wheelwright, Frank Westbrook, retired during the last war. The brickyard was closed down in 1912. The trade of blacksmith managed to survive, carried on at John Whitear's premises by Mr William Padwick and then by his nephew, Mr Walter Murphy, who made up for the decline in horse-shoeing by the repair of farm machinery and more latterly by ornamental ironwork. Thus most of the crafts have now disappeared, replaced only by the motor repair garage next to the former endowed schoolhouse, which began life in the early 1900s as a cycle shop.

The more social side of village life has experienced considerable change as well. The Vicar of Preston Candover is now also responsible for Bradley, Brown Candover and Northington. The school, rebuilt in 1964, is now a junior school and draws its pupils from these same parishes, their former schools having been closed down in turn over the past fifty years or more. The school continued to be used for social occasions until after the Great War when an army hut was acquired for use as a village hall. It was replaced by a modern building in the mid-1950s and this now accommodates many diverse activities: Over-Sixties Club, Women's Institute, Mother's Union, Guides, Youth Club, Gardening Club, Old Tyme Dancing, Dramatics Society and Playgroup. Behind the hall are tennis courts while up on the Wield Road is a recreation ground which came into being through the enclosure of Oakhills Common in 1870, and here the Cricket Club continues to uphold its long tradition.

Thus Preston Candover and Nutley are now very different in appearance and atmosphere from what they must have been in the 1850s. Certain buildings have gone, like Nutley Church, the school, the Croft, and the houses that belonged to George Allen, the Clark sisters, the Majors and the Parkers. A small council estate now stands on Allen's

92

Farm and the former Parish Cottage near Tulls Hill is used as a garage. Many other cottages do remain, though often restored to a condition and commanding a price which would have left their former occupants dumbfounded. Perhaps more evocative of the period though are the plaques and inscriptions in the church. At the base of each window are various dedications, many of them to members of the Wilson family but also to John-James and Charlotte King, Richard and Henrietta Purefoy Fitzgerald, as well as to George Allen and Young William Gardiner. The plaque in memory of Edward Wickham still hangs unobtrusively near the altar, and right down at the back of the pulpit is another in memory of Miss Harriet Blunt.

A very evocative spot is the old St Mary's churchyard where most of the graves now lie forgotten amidst the long grass, cow-parsley and nettles. Some familiar names can be discerned: John Thorp Senior and Junior, John Whitear, William Hutton, the Gardiner family, Joseph and Jane Allen and their son George. The grave of Maria Light, Daniel's first wife, is marked by a 'stone' of cast iron while in an elaborate and overgrown tomb lies Charlotte, the first wife of Farmer Bradby of Moundsmere. The Reverend Wickham and his wife Louisa lie against the chancel wall with the Reverend and Mrs Sumner Wilson close by. Two stones lodged against a yew tree belong to Albert and John Penton Major. Another stone, quite small and its surface flaking, reads: 'In memory of the beloved children of Charles & Ann Mercer'; they had six sons, none of whom lived more than a few weeks. And close by Tulls Lane beneath one of the yew trees lies Sabina, the wife of James Vine, her stone bearing an inscription from the Ninety-Fourth Psalm: 'But the Lord is my defence and my God is the rock of my refuge'. The stones of course mark the resting place of only the few. Somewhere in the churchyard must lie all those generations of Duffins, Lynches, Wiggs, Hopkins, Alexanders and all the other labouring families who were too poor to have any such memorial carved to the lives they spent in the Candover Valley.

93

Index

A – Greenway Field
B – Woodhouse Field
C – Burnell Field
D – Windmill Field
E – Little Field

Land held by
Widow Waltridge

NUTLEY

AXFORD

0   ½ Miles

The Common Fields of the Manor of Nutley in 1635

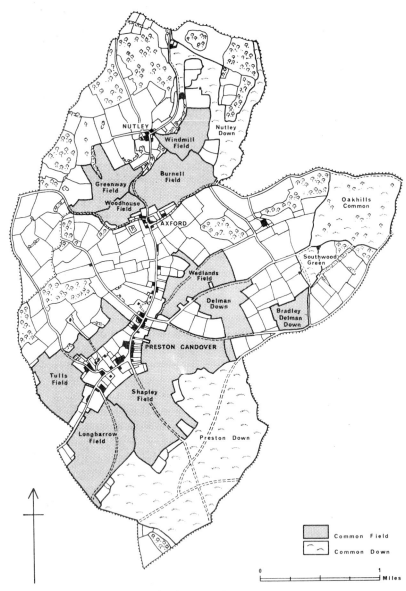

The Common Lands of Preston Candover and Nutley, 1820

NUTLEY

Nutley Down

Windmill Field

Burnell Field

Greenway Field

Woodhouse Field

AXFORD

Oakhills Common

Southwood Green

Wedlands Field

Delman Down

Bradley Delman Down

PRESTON CANDOVER

Tulls Field

Shapley Field

Longbarrow Field

Preston Down

Common Field

Common Down

0   1
Miles

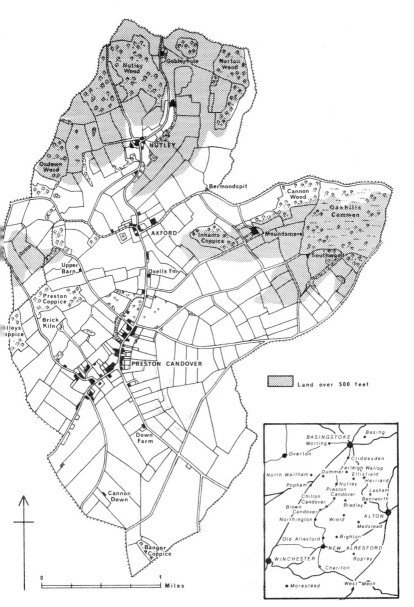

The parishes of Preston Candover and Nutley, 1851

Land over 500 feet

Nutley Wood
Gobleyhole
Nutlea Wood
Oxdown Wood
NUTLEY
Bermondspit
Cannon Wood
Oakhills Common
AXFORD
Inhams Coppice
Moundsmere
Southwood
Upper Barn
Oxells Fm.
Preston Coppice
Brick Kiln
...lleys ...oppice
PRESTON CANDOVER
Down Farm
Cannon Down
Bangor Coppice

0 ____ 1 Miles

BASINGSTOKE
Basing
Worting
Overton
Cliddesden
North Waltham
Farleigh Wallop
Dummer
Ellisfield
Herriard
Popham
Nutley
Chilton
Candover
Preston
Candover
Lasham
Bentworth
Bradley
ALTON
Brown
Candover
Northington
Wield
Medstead
Old Alresford
Bighton
NEW ALRESFORD
WINCHESTER
Ropley
Cheriton
Moorstead
West Meon

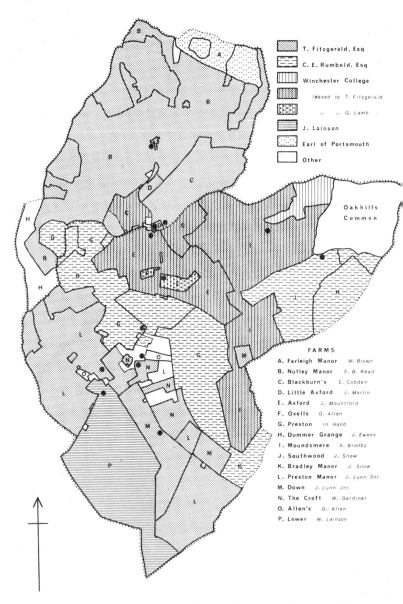

FARMS

A. Farleigh Manor   *W. Brown*
B. Nutley Manor   *E. B. Read*
C. Blackburn's   *E. Cobden*
D. Little Axford   *J. Martin*
E. Axford   *J. Mountford*
F. Oxells   *G. Allen*
G. Preston   *In Hand*
H. Dummer Grange   *J. Ewens*
I. Moundsmere   *A. Bradby*
J. Southwood   *J. Snow*
K. Bradley Manor   *J. Snow*
L. Preston Manor   *J. Lunn Snr*
M. Down   *J. Lunn Jnr*
N. The Croft   *W. Gardiner*
O. Allen's   *G. Allen*
P. Lower   *W. Lainson*

T. Fitzgerald, Esq
C. E. Rumbold, Esq
Winchester College
leased to T. Fitzgerald
" " *G. Lamb*
J. Lainson
Earl of Portsmouth
Other

Oakhills
Common

The major landowners in Preston Candover and Nutley, 1851

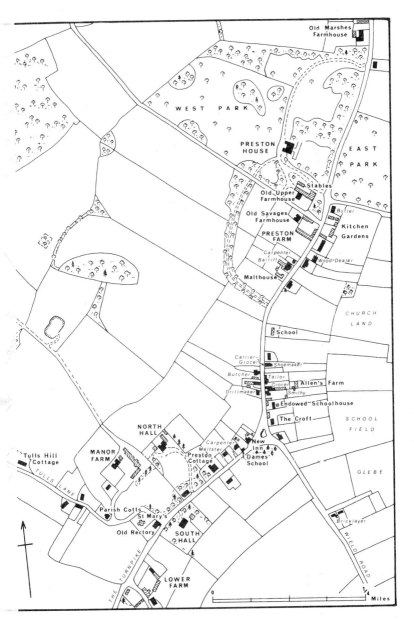

Preston Candover, 1851

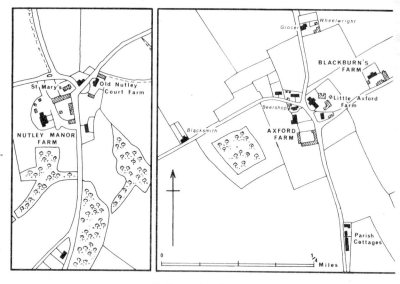

Nutley and Axford, 1851

These maps are based upon the Ordnance Survey map of 1870.